高校秘书学专业系列教材　总主编◎杨剑宇

U0095406

涉外秘书英语阅读

总主编◎杨剑宇　副总主编◎冯修文

主　编◎莫玉羚　周红宇　副主编◎吴连春　史妍青

编　者（排名不分先后）

莫玉羚　谭湘蓉　史妍青

严大为　吴连春　周红宇

李　雷　冯修文

华东师范大学出版社

涉外秘书专业本科系列教材编委会

总　序

涉外秘书是指在我国三资企业、外国驻华机构、我国涉外单位和部门等供职，辅助上司实施涉外经济活动或涉外事务管理的专门人才，是改革开放后产生的新型的外向型秘书。

涉外秘书要求能精通外语、操作办公自动化设备，懂经济、法律，掌握秘书工作理论和技能，了解和适应不同的中外文化环境，具有国际眼光，熟悉国际市场游戏规则，适应国际竞争的需要。

我国高校的秘书专业诞生于1980年。1984年起，在广东、上海、北京先后产生了涉外秘书专业。当时，有的称中英文秘书，有的称现代秘书等等。1996年，教育部高等教育自学考试办公室将涉外秘书作为一个独立的自考专业设置。同时，在成人高校也设立了涉外秘书专业，先是专科，后发展成既有专科，也有本科。众多高校也设置了涉外秘书专业的本科方向。2012年，秘书学专业被教育部列入本科目录，涉外秘书专业迎来又一个发展高潮。

专业建设，教材领先。我从上世纪80年代中期起在上海任教涉外秘书专业课程，教材是自编的讲义。从90年代起的一二十年中，先后应华侨出版社、湖北科技出版社、上海人民出版社之约，在讲义的基础上修改补充，弃旧增新，出版了几批涉外秘书专业的教材，包括全国自考统考的涉外秘书专业教材。计有《涉外秘书概论》《涉外秘书实务》《秘书和公共关系》《涉外秘书礼仪》《涉外秘书英语》《秘书英语》等。这些教材满足了高校师生教学的急需。但是，由于这几批教材是在讲义基础上产生的，难免存在局限性。尤其，涉外秘书专业的根本特性是涉外性，外语是涉外秘书的基本功，而这些教材除《涉外秘书英语》《秘书英语》外，全是中文写的。所以，我一直计划组织编写一套以英语为主的，更加适合实际需要的涉外秘书专业教材。

在华东师范大学出版社和上海建桥学院的支持下，这一计划得以实现。我们组织了从事涉外秘书专业教学多年、具有丰富经验的一线教师，编写成了这套教材，计有7册：《涉外秘书导论》《涉外秘书实务》《涉外秘书英语综合》《涉外秘书英语阅读》《涉外秘书英语写作》《涉外秘书英语听说》《涉外商务单证》。除《涉外秘书导论》和《涉外秘书实务》是用中文写的外，其余均用英语撰写。

掌握一门外语，是担任涉外秘书的基本条件。由于英语在世界上最为流行，因此，涉外秘书应当熟练地掌握英语。熟练地掌握英语，包括准确地听懂，流利地说清，快速地阅读，熟练地书写和翻译。涉外秘书工作的实践证明，仅学习、掌握普通英语是不够的。要胜任涉外秘书工作，还必须学习、掌握涉外秘书工作的职业英语。为此，我们针对涉外秘书工作的实际需要，在调查了解涉外秘书实际工作的基础上，编写了本系列教材，以满足师生的需要。

本系列教材的编写，遵循三个原则：实用；由浅入深；训练听、说、读、写、译能力。

实用是指本系列教材内容紧紧围绕涉外秘书的主要业务，如接听电话、接待来访、安排上司工作日程和商务旅行、筹办会议以及处理邮件、传真，拟写社交书信、贸易信函、经济合同等，对这些业务，本系列教材具有直接的指导作用。

由浅入深是指本系列教材的布局先从最简单的运用英语接听电话等开始，继而逐步深入，做到由易到难，循序渐进。

训练听、说、读、写、译能力，指本系列教材内容既有接听电话、接待来访等以训练听说能力为主的单元，也有传真、拟写社交书信、贸易信函、经济合同等以训练读写译为主的单元，还有筹办会议、应聘等综合训练听、说、读、写、译能力的单元。

同时，我们还组织编写了秘书学本科专业系列教材，其中的《文书处理和档案管理》、《秘书应用写作》、《管理学原理》、《秘书公关原理与实务》、《中国秘书史》、《秘书心理学》等教材，涉外秘书专业可以通用。这样，这套教材实际上共有13册，是至今最完整的名副其实的涉外秘书本科系列教材。

在本系列教材的出版过程中，华东师范大学出版社的李恒平、范耀华和姚望三位编辑给予了很大帮助，在此谨表谢意。

我们付出了努力，希望把这套教材尽可能编得好些。但是，由于涉外秘书尚是发展中的专业，加之我们水平有限，本系列教材不足之处在所难免，敬请广大读者指正。

本系列教材得到上海市扶持基金项目资助。

杨剑宇

2013 年 2 月

前　言

秘书学于2012年正式列入教育部本科目录,这是秘书界一件可喜可贺的大事。可喜之后,难免有点忧愁。那就是秘书学本科的教材建设,特别是秘书(本科)英语的教材建设。我们知道,教材作为"整个教育系统的软件",它不仅反映着社会发展的要求,同时在某种程度上还直接决定着受教育者的培养质量。因而,世界各国都非常重视教材的开发和建设。今日之秘书人才培养,不能再局限于"办文、办会、办事"能力,而是要立足现代开放型经济对秘书岗位能力的需要。由此可见,我们培养出的涉外秘书本科人才要具备较高的岗位英语应用能力才能胜任其岗位需要,尤其是涉外企事业单位秘书岗位所需的英语应用能力,这是未来秘书学本科涉外秘书英语教材建设的重点。基于此,由上海建桥学院秘书系牵头,华东师范大学出版社组织国内从事涉外秘书英语教学的一线骨干教师和企业涉外秘书岗位从业人员参与编写这套《涉外秘书英语系列丛书》,这套丛书的核心理念旨在培养涉外秘书岗位所需的英语应用能力。

本教材是《涉外秘书英语系列丛书》中的阅读教程。全书12个单元,旨在培养和提高涉外秘书岗位所需的管理能力,内容涉及:办公室管理、信息管理、业绩管理、会议管理、商务差旅管理、人事管理、现金管理、财务管理、营销管理、商务管理和管理创新等。每单元的内容选取和体例设置,围绕创新型人才能力培养展开。

PART A

选材是一篇文字浅显但非常幽默的趣味短文,幽默中蕴含管理理念。设置这部分内容旨在激发学生的学习兴趣,浅显的文章确保每位学生(即使英语基础不好)都能读得懂,幽默风趣的内容让每位学生都喜欢,同时在阅读后设置一些思考题启发学生,培养学生的思辨能力。

PART B & C

选取两篇与单元主题紧扣的文章,设置2—3个在阅读之前的讨论题,作为阅读导入;学生阅读后,再完成巩固练习。练习设置充分注意难易结合,基础知识与能力提高相互关照,关注每位学生的发展。

PART D

阅读技能培养。这部分介绍了常用的阅读策略,包括预测、略读、快速阅读、根据上下文推测词意、信息归纳、观点提取等。每种策略先做简要介绍,然后配有相关的练习,检验和巩固学生对该阅读策略的理解和掌握。

PART E

作为单元巩固阅读练习,既是单元核心内容的延展阅读,也为学生参加各类证书考试提供实战练习,比如托业考试、剑桥商务英语证书、剑桥商务秘书资格证书等。本单元的题型以上述与涉外秘书相关的岗位或资格证书考试的考纲来设置。

参与本教程筹划和编写人员,有来自高校的一线骨干教师,部分参编者还是双师型教师,曾在公司任职,有着丰富的实际操作经验和公司企业管理经验,还有来自一线岗位的外企涉外秘书人员。

涉外秘书(本科)教材的编写,还在不断的探索中,我们大胆地迈出第一步。在探索中前进,这其中肯定会有这样那样的不足,万望同仁和专家提出批评和指正。

编者

2012 年 12 月

Contents

Unit 5 Conference Management

Unit 6 Business Trip Management

Unit 7 HR Management

Unit 8 Cash Management

Unit 9　Financial Management

Unit 10　Marketing Management

Unit 11　Business Management

Unit 12　Management Innovation

Appendix

Unit 1
Office Management (I)

Matrix

- E-office
- Office manager

Part A Brainstorming

Directions: *Read the following short story and fill in the blank. And then discuss the following questions.*

➢ *What can you learn from the funny story?*
➢ *What do you think of the former CEO?*

Three Envelopes

A fellow had just been hired as the New CEO of a large high tech corporation. The CEO who was stepping down met with him privately and presented him with three numbered envelopes. "Open these if you run up against a problem you don't think you can solve," he said.

Well, things went along pretty smoothly. But six months later, sales took a downturn and he was really catching a lot of heat. About at his wit's end, he remembered the envelopes. He went to his drawer and took out the first envelope. The message read: "Blame your predecessor." The new CEO called a press conference and tactfully laid the blame at the feet of the previous CEO. Satisfied with his comments, the press and Wall Street responded positively. Sales began to pick up and the problem was soon behind him.

About a year later, the company was again experiencing a slight dip in sales, combined with serious product problems. Having learned from his previous experience, the CEO quickly opened the second envelope. The message read: "Reorganize." This he did, and the company quickly rebounded.

After several consecutive profitable quarters, the company once again fell on difficult times. The CEO went to his office, closed the door and opened the third envelope. The message said: "_____"

The following information may do help to expand your thinking perspective:

1. Why was the former CEO fired? And what was his experience of managing the company?

2. Product life cycle vs. Company life cycle

3. In your opinion, can a manager stay in his or her position for a lifetime? Why or why not?

Part B E-Office

Pre-reading Questions

➢ *What is E-office, OA (Office Automation) and Paperless Office?*

➢ *What are advantages and disadvantages of E-office?*

The electronic office, or e-office, was a term coined to cover the increasing use of computer-based information technology for office work, especially in the 1980s. It was a marketing buzzword at the time, but now it is not so widely used since all modern offices are electronic offices.

The term appeared much earlier in the name of the LEO computer (Lyons Electronic Office), that first ran a business application in 1951 in England.

The ongoing process that led to e-office adoption was elimination of paper and making most of the office communications electronic. The definition of electronic office is not precise, and it might be either:

➢ *the introduction of individual computers running office software applications, such as word processors,*

➢ *or the interconnection of office computers using a local area network (LAN),*

> *or the centralization of office functions via web applications.*

The introduction of e-office improved accuracy and efficiency of organizations and thereby improved their level of service, while theoretically lowering costs and drastically reducing the consumption of paper. Many documents are still being printed out and circulated on paper, however, especially the ones that require signature.

E-office can make the office work more efficient. However, every coin has two sides, sometimes we will complain that it is no more efficient with electronic communication than they were with paper. Here is a simple set of rules and suggestions to help secretaries deal with the barrage of e-mails that they receive.

One of the first issues that causes confusion with new e-mail users (and many veterans) is deciding on which line to place a recipient: To, cc, or bcc. When addressing a message, observe the following guidelines:

> **To**: *Put people on this line who are responsible for acting on information in the message body or to those from whom you expect a direct response. Unless the recipient is expected to do something as a result of receiving the mail, then don't put his/her name on the To line.*

> **CC**: *cc stands for courtesy copy. (E-mail history scholars will argue that this stands for carbon copy, but since none of us has ever gotten his or her hands dirty by reading an electronic piece of correspondence, it really doesn't seem appropriate to carry this 1970s metaphor forward.) This means that you're letting these people know about the contents of the message as a courtesy only and you do not expect them either to respond or to act on the basis of receiving the e-mail. In general, you should not hit Reply to All when responding to a cc message. Reply to All should only be used when responding to a message in which you're included on the To line. As a cc recipient, the sender of the message did not intend to engage you in a dialogue about the subject, but only intended for you to know as a courtesy.*

> **BCC**: *bcc means blind courtesy copy. This means that you want someone to know about a message, but you don't need or want the other respondents to know that others are receiving the message. The most common use for addresses on this line is: Doing broadcast mailings (Put yourself in the To line and all the broadcast recipients in the BCC line); Sending a mail to outside parties and alerting people inside the company that the message has been sent.*

Remember that if you put someone's e-mail address on the BCC line, then the external recipient doesn't have a copy of the e-mail address, but if you put them on the CC line then the external recipient has the e-mail address（potentially leading to more spam or people making contacts inside the company that were not intended to be allowed by the sender of the message）.

One final recommendation: Never send a response of five words or less unless the sender specifically requests a response from a predetermined list of choices.（Will you attend the meeting? Yes/No.）

If you're the only person on the To line, then it should be understood that if there are actions to take as a result of the message, then you'll take care of it. And if you're not going to, then it should require a more detailed response than "no" to explain and sending a response of "OK" or "I'll take care of it" is unnecessary.

Task One Choose the best answer to fill in the blank.

1. Digital is the _____ of the moment in communication technology.

   A. headline   B. deadline   C. buzzword   D. big word

2. As the champion of the Beijing Olympics, his _____ from the competition in the first round in London Olympics was a great surprise.

   A. limitation   B. elimination   C. delimitation   D. diminution

3. If you say that there is a/an _____ between two or more things, you mean that they are very closely connected.

   A. interconnection   B. internet   C. connection   D. relation

4. Every _____ has two sides, so it depends on you how to treat it.

   A. person   B. thing   C. note   D. coin

5. At the meeting, all the attendees lodged a _____ of complaints about the low salary.

   A. bag   B. barrage   C. bar   D. rage

6. Although she would not like to accept his invitation, she wrote a letter of thanks out of _____.

   A. recipient   B. revenge   C. courtesy   D. appreciation

7. _____ will be treated as spams or junk mails by receivers sometimes.

   A. Mailings by CC   B. Broadcast mailings

   C. Mailings without subject   D. Mailings by BCC

8. An alarm sounds when the temperature reaches a _____ level.

A. predetermined   B. determined   C. doomed   D. predicted

Task Two Decide whether the following statements are true or false according to the text.

. . . .

1. (   ) E-office is out of time because it has been replaced by more advanced technology.
2. (   ) E-office is paperless office.
3. (   ) E-office may sometimes make work less efficient.
4. (   ) Knowing how to deal with emails can make secretaries work more efficiently.
5. (   ) The external recipient cannot see the e-mail address on the BCC line.

Task Three Translate the following sentences from the text into Chinese.

. . . .

1. Many documents are still being printed out and circulated on paper, however, especially the ones that require signature.

_____

_____

2. Unless the recipient is expected to do something as a result of receiving the mail, then don't put his name on the To line.

_____

_____

3. As a CC recipient, the sender of the message did not intend to engage you in a dialogue about the subject, but only intended for you to know as a courtesy.

_____

_____

4. This means that you want someone to know about a message, but you don't need or want the other respondents to know that others are receiving the message.

_____

_____

5. If you're the only person on the To line, then it should be understood that if there are actions to

take as a result of the message, then you'll take care of it.

_____

_____

Part C Office Management

Pre-reading Questions

➢ *What responsibilities should an office manager take?*

➢ *What are office management functions?*

Office is a place in which business, clerical and professional activities take place. Management is executive ability to handle a business. Hence, office management is the administrative handling, controlling and maintaining a balanced process of work inside the office of an organization whether it's a big or small company/business, which is necessary to achieve the best service it can provide to the people who will receive a great benefit.

The office manager is the coordinator of the work system. An office manager is responsible for planning, organizing, and controlling the clerical aspect of the organization, including the preparation, communication, coordination and storage of data to support production and other important operations of an industrial establishment. Often they also engage in marketing. Also, their tasks are to monitor the work processes and to evaluate the outcome. The outcomes of work are intended for what can be called the final receiving system, for instance, clients, customers, and other departments.

Furthermore, their role is to coordinate on the front end by issuing various assignments. They usually lead or manage a team of secretaries or administrative clerks. And they take care of the assignment of tasks within the department, but the more complex tasks tend to come to their desk.

Positions allocated to usual classification perform a combination of the following office management functions:

➢ *Budget development and implementation*

➢ *Purchasing*

➢ *Book keeping*

- Human resources
- Accounting
- Printing
- Records management
- Forms management
- Payroll
- Facilities management
- Space management
- Risk management
- Grants administration
- Affirmative action and equal employment opportunity
- Information technology and telecommunications
- Monitoring the management of health and safety in the company office
- Assisting senior managers in identifying health and safety needs in their departments
- Responsibility for the day to day running of the office
- Liaising with senior managers to ensure that staff in the division have appropriate information technology equipment
- Managing a range of budgets including accommodation, health & safety for company
- Planning, consulting and managing office moves for the division and other units within the department

Considering the diversity of functions, someone holding an office manager position is expected to have many talents. Some of the competencies which he is expected to possess are problem solving and decision making abilities, integrity, assertiveness, flexibility, accuracy and the ability to cope with pressure.

Task One Fill in the blanks with the expressions given below. Change the form when necessary.

. . . .

clerical; executive; coordinator; engage in; administrative; payroll; liaise with; competency; integrity; assertiveness

1. Whether at work or at home, our goal is to _____ activities that are both personally significant

and enjoyable.

2. During the economic depression, some of the _____ staff were eased off to cut down expense.

3. The Product Manager has to _____ people in all those areas during the entire life cycle of the product.

4. Other industries have had to sack managers to reduce _____ cost.

5. After the reform and opening-up, Chinese are becoming more and more _____ in the international communication.

6. Some firms require candidates to complete personality and _____ tests benchmarked according to what an employer considers to be some key traits for a particular role.

7. They have 100,000 employees on the _____ .

8. She has climbed up to the office manager from the _____ staff after ten years' hard work.

9. I am honored to recommend Tom Su, a man of _____ , who deals with everything in a moral and honest way.

10. The campaign needs an effective _____ to unite all the departments together and run efficiently.

Task Two Choose the best answer according to the text.

1. From the text we can learn that _____ .

   A. office management is of great importance

   B. the office manager plays an important coordinating role of the work system

   C. the office manager is as important as the general manager

   D. the office manager is versatile

2. The word "flexibility" means _____ .

   A. ability to work efficiently

   B. personality of respecting others both in high and low positions

   C. characteristics of getting along with others well

   D. ability to change to suit new conditions or situations

3. Why is the office manager the coordinator of the work system?

   A. The office manager's work is very important.

   B. The office manager's position is indispensable in the company.

   C. The office management functions cover almost all the departments of the company.

   D. Office management is quite a managing buzzword nowadays.

4. Which of the following management functions is not for the office manager?

A. Office move.

B. Health and safety for the staff at work.

C. Company developing strategies.

D. Equal employment opportunity.

5. A potential candidate for the office manager is the one who _____.

A. graduated from a key university at least with an MBA degree

B. is upright, adaptable, positive, and strong-minded

C. must ever work as an office clerk

D. boasts problem-solving and marketing abilities

Task Three Sum up the main idea of the text in 100 words.

Part D Reading Strategy

Predicting

Predicting in reading is a strategy the reader uses to guess the content of the text based on contextual clues and prior knowledge. It is an ongoing process that engages one's attention when reading. One must think in advance about what is coming next (making new predictions), then confirm or revise predictions based on evidence in the text. Skilled readers use both textual clues as well as prior knowledge to make predictions. Good readers constantly think about their predictions to confirm or revise them. You may make predictions before reading, while reading and after reading.

Before reading: One can make predictions about what the text likely contains based on information such as the heading, subheading, illustrations, charts, graphs, or maps, as well as prior knowledge of the topic. One may say:

> ➢ I think ...
> ➢ I bet ...
> ➢ I wonder if ...
> ➢ I imagine ...
> ➢ I suppose ...
> ➢ I predict ...
> ➢ I think this text will be about ...

While reading: Gather evidence from the text that supports or disproves previous predictions.

After reading: Confirm or refine predictions by using information found in the text.

Methods and Principles of Risk Management

Methods

For the most part, these methods consist of the following elements, performed, more or less, in the following order.

> ➢ identify, characterize, and assess threats;
> ➢ assess the vulnerability of critical assets to specific threats;
> ➢ determine the risk (i. e. the expected likelihood and consequences of specific types of attacks on specific assets);
> ➢ identify ways to reduce those risks;
> ➢ prioritize risk reduction measures based on a strategy.

Principles of risk management

The International Organization for Standardization (ISO) identifies the following principles of risk management:

> ➢ create value-resources expended to mitigate risk should be less than the consequence of inaction, or (as in value engineering), the gain should exceed the pain;

- ➢ be an integral part of organizational processes;
- ➢ be part of decision making;
- ➢ explicitly address uncertainty and assumptions;
- ➢ be systematic and structured;
- ➢ be based on the best available information;
- ➢ be tailorable;
- ➢ take into account human factors;
- ➢ be transparent and inclusive;
- ➢ be dynamic, iterative and responsive to change;
- ➢ be capable of continual improvement and enhancement;
- ➢ be continually or periodically re-assess.

Follow-up Work Please review your predictions of the text above by completing the following statements.

1. My prediction was correct because _____ .
2. My prediction was incorrect because _____ .
3. My prediction was partially correct because _____ .

Part E Banked Cloze

Direction: In the following text, there are ten blanks. Read the text and then fill in each blank with a word from the word bank. Each choice in the bank is identified by a letter. Do not use any of the words more than twice.

Office Politics

Office politics _____ (1) from office gossip in that people participating in office politics do so with the objective of gaining advantage, whereas gossip can be a purely social activity. However, the activities are related. Office gossip is often used by an individual to place themselves at a point where they can control the flow of information and therefore gain _____ (2) advantage.

At the root of office politics is the issue of manipulation which can happen in any relationship where one or more of the parties _____ (3) use indirect means to achieve their goals. In the workplace, where resources are limited, individuals have an incentive to achieve their goals at the expense of their colleagues. For example, if six people apply for one promotion, they might expect the selection to be made purely on _____ (4). When one of the people who has anything but merits believes that this would put him at a disadvantage, he may use other means of coercion or influence to put himself into an _____ (5) position.

The aims of office politics or manipulation in the workplace are not always increased pay or a _____ (6). Often, the goal may simply be greater power or control for its own end; or to repudiate a competitor. While office politics do not necessarily aim at _____ (7) gains — they can be a means towards outcomes which benefit the company.

Office politics is part of being human, reflecting the reality of human _____ (8). For example, people are generally favorably biased towards people they know, like and trust, even when they are trying to be _____ (9).

People who hate politics think they have to change who they are to succeed. Well, anyone who is being their best self — kind, considerate, expressive, interested in others — will do fine in office politics. So get to know yourself. Saying you just can't do politics is giving up on being your best _____ (10).

A) advantageous	B) differs	C) impartial	D) involved	E) maximum
F) merits	G) nature	H) promotion	I) self	J) selfish

Unit 2
Office Management (II)

Matrix

· Office control
· Interpersonal relationship

Part A   Brainstorming

Directions: *Read the following short story and fill in the blank. And then discuss the following questions.*

➤ *What can you learn from the following story?*
➤ *Why did cannibals prefer to eat leaders and managers?*

Don't Eat a Person Who is Working

Five cannibals (man eaters) get appointed as programmers in an IT company.

During the welcoming ceremony the boss says, "You'll all be part of our team now. You can earn good money here, and you can go to the company canteen for something to eat. So don't trouble the other employees."

Four weeks later the boss returns and says, "You're all working very hard, and I'm very satisfied with all of you. One of our developers has disappeared however. Do any of you know what happened to her?" The cannibals disown all knowledge of the missing developer.

After the boss has left, the leader of the cannibals says to the others, "Which of you idiots ate the developer?"

One of the cannibals raises his hand hesitantly, to which the leader of the cannibals says, "You FOOL! For four weeks we've been eating team leaders, managers, and project managers and no one has noticed anything. And now you ate one developer and it got noticed. So hereafter please don't eat _____ ."

The following information may do help to expand your thinking perspective：

1. Why did the boss find the developer disappear?

2. In your opinion, who is at work actually in a company?

Part B Office Control

Pre-reading Questions

➤ *What does office control include?*

➤ *Why is office control important for an organization?*

Office control can ensure that office working standards and procedures are being maintained and any deviations corrected. It includes the controls for attendance checking, staff leave, office safety and security, office stresses and crisis management and so on. To deal with such office matters, use a specific and easy-to-follow procedures manual to give clear, step-by-step instructions as to how to deal with a particular task. In order to review procedures and amend them if necessary, an office audit is carried out.

Attendance Checking

To help keep track of employee attendance, time recorder systems, including electronic employee time clocks, time recorders and time and date stamps are used in the office to allow for accurate employee attendance records.

Staff Leave

Staff may be absent for a number of reasons. Either they take leave, or it is public holiday or their family members are ill, or they attend training or meeting. It is a good idea to display some types of wall planner or a leave calendar on which to record leave when the dates have been agreed. This information will also be recorded in a diary which is held centrally either in a book or on computer so that all members of staff have access to it. Staff intending to leave may need to complete a Staff Leave Form giving details for the leave.

Office Safety

In order to avoid the unsafe practices and reduce stress in the office, a secretary should design office policies and give personal presentations to teach and remind others of the use of safe working methods and equipment. Office workers have a duty to take reasonable care for the health of themselves and of others. If there are already some office risks in the office, take some steps to reduce the risks.

The secretary should put notices of fire evacuation, first aid, machine operation and general office safety at public places to remind staff of emergency precautions and actions to be taken when an emergency occurs.

If accidents and emergencies happen, a secretary should report and record immediately by using the formal accident report form to give some detailed explanation to it for reference or evidence purpose in the future.

Security Inspection

To monitor and maintain office security, a secretary needs to effectively maintain and evaluate the incoming and outgoing manual or electronic mails; reception of visitors; record-keeping systems for personal identification, entrance and exits.

There is a wide selection of security equipment and supplies and security system including video surveillance systems, hidden camera kits, photo ID systems, metal detectors, digital voice recorders, portable receiver recording systems, transmitters, wireless accessories, video motion detection systems, VCRs, and emergency lights that can be used for office safety. While choosing proper equipment or application, you should consult expertise.

Office Stresses

If steps are taken, office risks are often avoidable, but there are some kind of risks and dangers that are not visible, such as work-related stress. Proper management of stress is important to office administrators. These office stresses usually cover three types: job stresses, psychological stresses and technological stresses.

Technological stressors include inadequate training; old, poorly maintained equipment or tools; pace of workload; lack of right equipment or tools and unsafe or poorly designed equipment.

Crisis Management

In time of security or other crisis for the office, some decisions need to be made:

➢ What common office activities should be delayed or dropped at the moment as a result of the crisis?

➢ What, if any, issues or activities now deserve much greater office attention?

➢ What changes should the office make in staffing to accommodate these changes in the environment?

➢ How will the office communicate these changes to office staff?

Task One Choose the best answer to fill in the blank.

· ·

1. The number of the _____ will run to eighty.

   A. abundance   B. attendance   C. importance   D. significance

2. They suffered huge losses in the financial _____.

   A. growth   B. period   C. boom   D. crisis

3. I think we should work out a strategy to _____ this situation.

   A. together with   B. agree with   C. deal with   D. study with

4. Let's _____ the figures and see what we have.

   A. play   B. display   C. replay   D. cosplay

5. Orders went out to prepare for the _____ of the city.

   A. evacuation   B. separation

   C. determination   D. vaccination

6. Lightweight teams cannot exist with occasional communication. They need continuous access to business _____.

   A. experience   B. experiment   C. expertise   D. expense

7. Police officers have been closely _____ the organization's activities.

   A. simulating   B. monitoring

   C. maintaining   D. communicating

8. An alarm sounds when the temperature reaches a level. You _____ a reward for being so helpful.

   A. determine   B. deserve   C. deceive   D. desire

Task Two Decide whether the following statements are true or false according to the text.

＇・・・・・・・・・・・・・・・・・・・・・・・・・・・・・・

1. (   ) An office audit is unnecessary for office control.
2. (   ) Time recorder systems can keep track of accurate employee attendance.
3. (   ) Staff may be absent for a number of reasons without completing a Staff Leave Form giving details for the leave.
4. (   ) Office stresses usually cover three types: job stresses, psychological stresses and technological stresses.
5. (   ) If accidents and emergencies happen, a secretary should report and record immediately.

Task Three Translate the following sentences from the text into Chinese.

・・・・・・・・・・・・・・・・・・・・・・・・・・・・

1. Office control can ensure that office working standards and procedures are being maintained and any deviations corrected.

_____

_____

2. Staff intending to leave may need to complete a Staff Leave Form giving details for the leave.

_____

_____

3. Office workers have a duty to take reasonable care for the health of themselves and of others.

_____

_____

4. These office stresses usually cover three types: job stresses, psychological stresses and technological stresses.

_____

_____

5. Technological stressors include inadequate training; old, poorly maintained equipment or tools; pace of workload; lack of right equipment or tools and unsafe or poorly designed equipment.

_____

Part C Interpersonal Relationship

Pre-reading Questions

➢ *What are important elements of a secretary's success?*

➢ *How to deal with relationship between the executive and secretary?*

An important element of a secretary's success and value to the executive lies in her/his skill in dealing with people, and in creating an impression which will enhance the organization's reputation. A good relationship with your coworkers and executives can make for a healthy career. Moreover, what makes an organization work better is relationships that are positive, co-operative and respectful. In this way everyone works for the good of the whole and towards a common purpose, which demands effective relationships based on mutual understanding.

Working with Colleagues

You will find the following suggestions very useful if you try to construct good relationships with other office members.

➢ Treat others with respect

Respect is the core of any good relationship. We show respect by listening to others and trying to understand how they view things. Quickly forming judgments based on prejudice is the complete opposite of respect. You can respect people (even if you find their behavior difficult to understand) by acknowledging that they are doing the best they can when their circumstances and history are taken into account.

➢ Accept differences

You will come in contact with many different people in an office. Their backgrounds and interests may be quite different from yours. You may not understand many of these people at first. And, because you don't understand them, you may dislike or disapprove of them. As a successful secretary, you need to accept other employees without judging them. You should recognize and respect people who are different from you. If you sincerely listen to others, you will learn more about them and avoid conflicts that result from a lack of understanding.

> Be willing to cooperate

You should have a cooperative attitude in working with other employees in the office since few jobs are performed in isolation and cooperation is necessary in order to attain（达到）company goals. You should willingly assist other employees in meeting job deadlines when the situation demands.

> Show your fairness

A fair person does not take advantage of others. For example, you may get an idea from someone else, but if you are fair, you will not take credit for the idea. Instead, you will give credit to the individual who gave you the idea. You also assume your share of responsibility without attempting to get your co-workers to do jobs that are yours.

Getting along with Executives

The secretary has a special relationship with her/his immediate executive because they work closely together in a "partnership" to achieve the objectives required of the executive's position. The secretary should, therefore, seek to serve the organization to the best of her/his ability, understand and appreciate the role of each executive and play her/his part in contribution towards the overall efficiency and smooth-working of the organization. Co-operation and respect are important in establishing successful relationships between secretaries and their seniors.

The qualities which make an ideal relationship between the executive and secretary are described as follows:

> The secretary should understand that it may be necessary to stay late if there is an urgent job to do; Nevertheless, the executive should not always expect the secretary to be in the office after hours when the work is not of an urgent nature.

> There must be a clear understanding about the scope of the work the secretary should undertake in the executive's absence and the executive should be perfectly satisfied that the secretary can cope with the work which may arise when the executive is not there.

> The secretary should be able to maintain the executive's confidential and private matters since he/she has easier access to confidential information.

> The secretary should be kept fully informed of everything that the executive is doing so that the secretary can be of most use to the executive.

> The secretary should set a high standard of conduct and efficiency for the rest of the office staff.

Task One   Fill in the blanks with the expressions given below. Change the form when necessary.

---

executive；*mutual*；*acknowledge*；*disapprove of*；*isolation*；*take advantage of*；*contribution*；*efficiency*；*nevertheless*；*confidential*

---

1. We hope you can _____ your mistake in public.

2. Don't consider the facts in _____ from others.

3. He was an author whose works were so little known as to be almost _____ .

4. Negotiations between unions and management are made more difficult by _____ distrust.

5. He has made an important _____ to the company's success.

6. I would like to say how much I _____ taking such an unnecessary step.

7. The _____ manager tossed out my application.

8. We can't take your advice. _____ , thank you for putting it.

9. He never helps me without trying to _____ me.

10. The two companies consolidated for greater _____ .

Task Two   Choose the best answer according to the text.

. . . .

1. Relationships that are _____ can make an organization work better.

   A. negative and offensive

   B. careful and cautious

C. positive, co-operative and respectful

D. selective, ambitious and considerate

2. _____ is the core of any good relationship.

A. Cooperation   B. Respect

C. Trust   D. Friendship

3. The word "prejudice" means _____ .

A. an attitude of admiration or esteem

B. a greeting or reception

C. a feeling of anger caused by being offended

D. a partiality that prevents objective consideration of an issue or situation

4. The text mainly talks about _____ .

A. some important elements of a secretary's success

B. the importance of working with colleagues

C. the importance of getting along with executives

D. the importance of mutual understanding

5. Which of the following qualities is NOT for making an ideal relationship between the executive and secretary?

A. The secretary should understand that it may be necessary to stay late if there is an urgent job to do.

B. The secretary may leak the executive's confidential and private matters since he/she has easier access to confidential information.

C. The secretary should be kept fully informed of everything that the executive is doing so that the secretary can be of most use to the executive.

D. The secretary should set a high standard of conduct and efficiency for the rest of the office staff.

Task Three Sum up the main idea of the text in 100 words.

. . . .

_____

_____

_____

_____

Part D Reading Strategy

Skimming

Skimming means very fast reading. When you skim, you read to get the main idea of a text and a few, but not all, of the details in that text. Skimming gives the fastest speed possible while maintaining a level of comprehension lower than that obtained at average reading speeds. In average reading the reader omits no part of the reading material. In the skimming, however, the reader selectively omits parts of the reading material.

Here is how to skim.

➢ Read the first paragraph or two in its entirety at the fastest average rate to grasp the idea of the story, the setting, a little of the author's style. Frequently an author will give an introduction in the first few paragraphs, presenting an overall picture of the selection.

➢ Move your eyes quickly over the third or fourth paragraph for the key sentence, picking up one or two important words, phrases, or numbers.

➢ Attempt to get the main idea of every paragraph plus a few facts. If the main idea is not summarized in any one sentence, try to detect the main idea from several sentences. Read slowly the part that indicates the needed main idea.

➢ Avoid the details in order to maintain the maximum skimming speed.

Fol l ow-up Work **Skim the following passage and then answer the questions briefly within 2 minutes.**

I have been very lucky to have won the Nobel Prize twice. It is, of course, very exciting to have such an important recognition of my work, but the real pleasure was in the work itself. Scientific research is like an exploration or a voyage of discovery. You are continually trying out new things that have not been done before. Many of them will lead nowhere and you have to try something different, but sometimes an experiment does work and tells you something new that is really exciting. However small the new finding may be, it is great to think "I am the only person who know this", and then you will have the fun of thinking what this finding will lead to and of deciding what will be the next experiment. One of the best things about scientific research is that you are always doing something different and it is never boring. There are good times when things go well and bad times when they don't. Some people get discouraged at the difficult times but when I have a failure my policy has always been not to worry but to start planning the next experiment , which is always fun.

1. What is the main idea of the paragraph?

_____

_____

2. What's the author's view of scientific experiment?

_____

_____

· ·

Part E Banked Cloze

Direction: *In the following text, there are ten blanks. Read the text and then fill in each blank with a word from the word bank. Each choice in the bank is identified by a letter. Do not use any of the words more than twice.*

How to Deal with Disagreements and Conflicts

Today's workplace is rather _____ (1), prompting disagreements that can impede work progress. Too often, people at work take their anxieties and unease out on one another. But conflicts at work need to be resolved so that productivity can flourish. It requires much tact, wisdom and practice of secretaries.

If you can take a positive and _____ (2) approach to the conflict situation, the few guidelines offered below may help you establish or reestablish a work environment that is healthier, happier and more productive for everyone.

Facing up to problems, don't let problems "fester"

Some of the biggest and most ugly interpersonal problems at work started small and were either deliberately or unconsciously _____ (3). Simple shyness or lack of assertive skills can allow a small interpersonal problem to grow. Address the problem when you are feeling relatively good about your colleague rather than waiting for the last _____ (4), which breaks the camel's back. Your approach should be calmer, more _____ (5) and more productive.

Get help if necessary

When dispute or conflict happened, _____ (6) is not easily to be achieved between the two parties involved. A third party, particularly one who is neutral and not simply taking your side, can help you develop a problem solving strategy, or may play an active _____ (7) role. Always be sure to find appropriate person for assistance solving problems immediately.

Talk about yourself and avoid the temptation to bully

"I" statements mean you are taking _____ (8) for your contributions to the problems, and for their solutions. You can use them to avoid the appearance of blaming the other party. Talk about how you feel, what you want, and what you are willing and trying to do. Last but not least, avoid the _____ (9) to bully. When you are angry or frustrated, it is easy to react aggressively, and try to force your colleagues to act as you think they should. Keep it in your mind, appealing to authority figures can only _____ (10) a conflict situation that makes it even worse.

A) ignored	B) mediator	C) constructive	D) temptation	E) inflame
F) responsibility	G) rational	H) stressful	I) straw	J) reconcilement

Unit 3
Information Management

Matrix

· **Recording and storing information**
· **Keeping information safe**

Part A Brainstorming

Directions: *Read the following short story and fill in the blank. And then discuss the following questions.*

· ·

➢ *What can you learn from the funny story?*
➢ *Why will misused technology lead to serious consequences?*

E-mail Errors

It's wise to remember how easily this wonderful technology can be misused, sometimes unintentionally, with serious consequences.

Consider the case of the Illinois man who left the snow-filled streets of Chicago for a vacation in Florida. His wife was on a business trip and was planning to meet him after the next day. When he reached his hotel, after checking in, he decided to send his wife a quick e-mail. Unable to find the scrap of paper on which he had written her e-mail address, he did his best to type it in from memory.

Unfortunately, he missed one letter, and his mail was directed instead to an elderly preacher's wife, whose husband had passed away only the day before. When the grieving widow checked her e-mail, she took one look at the monitor, let out a piercing scream, and fell to the floor in a dead faint.

At the sound, her family rushed into the room and saw this note on the screen:

_____.

The following information may do help to expand your thinking perspective:

1. Why did the man send the e-mail to the wrong address?

2. Would you commit an error unintentionally leading to serious consequences?

Part B Recording and Storing Information

Pre-reading Questions

➢ *What kinds of information will be kept in an office? Can you name some?*

➢ *What are the advantages and disadvantages of computer filling system?*

An important function of the office is to keep and search information, which may be stored on paper, disk or film, and ensuring quick and reliable access. A document filed incorrectly can be the cause of a delay in a business transaction, resulting in frustration and irritation to the staff concerned, and it may even contribute to the cancellation of an important contract. Only when the filing system is efficient can the office function properly. A failure to retrieve information when it is required will have serious repercussions for all sections of a business.

In large firms there may be a central filing system into which all documents are stored, with individual personalized filing by secretaries of their employers' papers. In a small firm, the secretary will be responsible for most of the filing of her employer's papers.

Recording

Records, whether they are in their original paper form or processed electronically, must be filed accurately so that they can be retrieved instantly. Benefits brought by efficient means of storage and retrieval of information are listed as below:

➢ It is quick and easier to locate information well-filed in an organized system.

➢ It is less likely that papers and documents will be mislaid or lost if they are filed regularly.

➢ Fire hazard can be decreased when multiple sheets of paper and documents left lying around are minimized.

➢ Queries can be answered quickly using accurate information.

> Information can be found quickly for reference purposes.

> Time which would be wasted searching through multiple documents and sheets of paper is saved.

> An efficient image is presented to the enquirer.

Types of Information

Following are types of information kept in an office:

> Customer details.

> Queries, orders and requests, and contracts.

> Index cards, catalogs, brochures, and reference books.

> Staff handbook containing office procedures and manuals.

> Internal and external telephone directories.

> Statistical returns, graphs, and charts.

> Plans, photographs, and videotext information.

> Trade journals and advertising materials.

> Old files which need to be kept for a certain period of time.

Filing

Nowadays, developments in electronic data storage have revolutionized the speed of retrieval and allowed greater and easier access to vast quantities of records without the need to store papers into bulky filing cabinets. That means information can be stored with the help of computerized filing system.

In computerized filing system, information is kept by using different types of software packages such as database and spreadsheet. Information can also be stored on other forms of computer-based storage such as floppy disk, network location, CD-ROM, etc. , according to different purposes or conditions.

Advantages of computer filing system:

> Speed of retrieval: information stored on network systems can be easily and quickly retrieved and located by staff in different departments.

> Space-effective: disks and CD-ROMs can store large amount of information.

> Easy updating.

> Paperwork-reduction: a considerable amount of paper work can be reduced.

> Greater security by using passwords.

> Files are not removed when access is made to them.

Disadvantages of computer filing system:

> Knowledge-requirement: staff need to have certain knowledge of computer to operate or access this system.

> Expensive equipment is required.

> It takes time to input data and verify it using a keyboard.

> Information loss: information can be corrupted by viruses.

> The danger of an operator accidentally erasing data from the memory of a computer.

> Back-up paper copies are needed, which increases the amount of material to be stored.

> Information can not be retrieved when there is a power cut or a system breakdown.

Task One Choose the best answer to fill in the blank.

. . . .

1. It's healthier to release _____ than to bottle it up.

   A. revolution   B. temptation   C. frustration   D. satisfaction

2. She tried to _____ the situation by making profuse apologies.

   A. receive   B. achieve   C. relieve   D. retrieve

3. What _____ will the war have on the economy?

   A. connections   B. constructions   C. repercussions   D. preventions

4. In no way am I _____ what has happened.

   A. stand for   B. responsible for   C. in charge of   D. approve of

5. Hearsay definitely can't be regarded as _____ information.

   A. accurate   B. detailed   C. reasonable   D. selective

6. She is sorting _____ into alphabetical order.

   A. references   B. queries   C. brochures   D. index cards

7. Some aircraft are designed to carry _____ freight or vehicles.

   A. stocky   B. tight   C. bulky   D. loose

8. Before the bank was willing to lend him money, it had to _____ that he was the true owner of the house.

   A. verify   B. identify   C. purify   D. clarify

Task Two Decide whether the following statements are true or false according to the text.

. . . .

1. (　　) A document filed correctly can be the cause of a delay in a business transaction, resulting in frustration and irritation to the staff concerned.
2. (　　) In a small firm, there may be a central filing system into which all documents are stored.
3. (　　) With efficient filing, information can be found quickly for reference purposes.
4. (　　) Nowadays, we still need to store large amounts of paper documents into bulky filing cabinets in spite of the developments in electronic data storage.
5. (　　) Even with the computer filing system, back-up paper copies are still needed, which increases the amount of material to be stored.

Task Three Translate the following sentences from the text into Chinese.

. . . .

1. Only when the filing system is efficient can the office function properly.

_____

_____

2. Records, whether they are in their original paper form or processed electronically, must be filed accurately so that they can be retrieved instantly.

_____

_____

3. Time which would be wasted searching through multiple documents and sheets of paper is saved.

_____

_____

4. In computerized filing system, information is kept by using different types of software packages such as database and spreadsheet.

_____

_____

5. Information will not be able to be retrieved when there is a power cut or a system breakdown.

_____

_____

Part C Keeping Information Safe

Pre-reading Questions

➢ *What is the importance of information to an organization?*

➢ *How to deal with information and prevent it from being breached or leaked?*

Information is important to an organization. Care has to be taken to keep information secure and to ensure that it is not lost, stolen, or left lying around, as applied to both paper and computerized information. It is essential that those who deal with information and records (usually the secretary takes such responsibility) should be aware of their responsibilities and constantly alert to any attempts made to breach confidentiality and leak information. Any suspicious circumstances must be reported to higher authority.

Security of Paper Documents

Awareness should be raised to develop good working habits when dealing with paper-based records:

➢ Documents should be filed immediately. Don't leave them on desks.

➢ Documents should be stored in fireproof cabinets.

➢ Filing cabinets should be kept locked.

➢ Office doors and desk drawers should be locked when you leave your office.

➢ Never leave confidential records lying around when you leave your office. Be sure to lock them away when they are not in use.

➢ If confidential documents have to be reproduced on a copier, it may be desirable for the secretary to do this to ensure that the contents are not disclosed to others.

➢ Remove the original copies from the glass plate in the photocopier immediately on completion of copying.

➢ Information/files should be released only to authorized members of staff and a signature obtained.

- Any confidential or secret documents no longer required should not be put in the waste paper bin but destroyed in a shredder.
- When faxing confidential information, ensure the receiving equipment has secrecy facilities. If not, telephone the addressee prior to faxing so that he or she is waiting at the fax machine to collect the information.

Security of Computerized Documents

Special attention should be paid to safeguard computerized data against information loss or leakage.

- Keep back-up duplicate copies of disks in a secure place.
- Keep the password confidential and changed frequently.
- Use codes, known only to users, for document file access.
- Use write-protect tags on system disks against attacks or alteration and do the multiple backups when necessary daily, weekly, monthly or quarterly.
- Take as much care over confidential computerized data and recorded data on dictation machines as you would with documents.
- Inform your manager immediately of any breaches of security you see or which are brought to your attention.
- Security should be the first concern for anyone who's connected to the Internet. When you set up a network, consider the security of every possible access point that is left exposed to attacks by hackers. Install firewall software and keep it up to date on every computer on your network.

Attention should also be paid to ensure computer security.

- Properly place the computer, lest the screen be read by visitors or passers-by.
- Scroll up the page quickly, or switch off VDU (Visual Display Unit) if a visitor approaches.
- Never leave confidential printouts on the desk.
- Check with your supervisor before sending information to anyone who asks for it.
- Computers may have an alarm system fitted to warn off potential thieves.
- Scan for virus frequently, and it is essential to always keep backup copies of work.
- Exit programs correctly and close off applications when leaving the desk.
- Save data regularly and store disks correctly.

Task One   Fill in the blanks with the expressions given below. Change the form when necessary.

· ·

breach; leak; suspicious; duplicate; lest; shredder; switch off; potential; warn off; regularly

1. I'm _____ of the government's intentions.
2. Be sure to _____ the light when you leave the office.
3. He picked up the agenda sheets and fed them into a _____ .
4. If you cannot come to term with it, eventually you will _____ the policies and be forced to leave the business in disgrace.
5. We meet _____ to discuss business.
6. He opened the door with a _____ key.
7. He denied that he had _____ the news to the press.
8. The road was closed to traffic after the accident, and the police were _____ everyone.
9. We dare not play jokes on him _____ he should become angry.
10. The dispute has scared away _____ investors.

Task Two   Choose the best answer according to the text.

· ·

1. Which of the following behaviors is NOT right for Security of Paper Documents?
   A. Documents should be filed immediately.
   B. Leave documents on desks.
   C. Documents should be stored in fireproof cabinets.
   D. Filing cabinets should be kept locked.

2. Any confidential or secret documents no longer required should be put in the _____ .
   A. waste paper bin   B. drawer
   C. shredder   D. filing cabinet

3. The word "confidential" means _____ .
   A. widely known or commonly encountered

B. worthy of notice

C. showing concern for the rights and feelings of others

D. of information given in confidence or in secret

4. Which of the following behaviors is NOT right for Security of Computerized Documents?

A. Keep back-up duplicate copies of disks in a secure place.

B. Keep the password confidential but never changed.

C. Use codes, known only to users, for document file access.

D. Use write-protect tags on system disks against attacks.

5. Which of the following attention should NOT be paid to ensure computer security?

A. Save data occasionally.

B. Computers may have an alarm system fitted to warn off potential thieves.

C. Exit programs correctly and close off applications when leaving the desk.

D. Properly place the computer, lest the screen be read by visitors or passers-by.

Task Three **Sum up the main idea of the text in 100 words.**

_____

_____

_____

_____

Part D Reading Strategy

Scanning

Scanning means looking for the exact answer to a specific question. It is a reading technique used when one wishes to locate a single fact or a specific piece of information with speed and accuracy.

Unlike shimming in which we know little or nothing about the material beforehand, scanning is often done when we know what we want to find. The goal is to find it quickly. In scanning a telephone directory, for example, we know the name of the person and that the directory is arranged alphabetically according to last names. Much of the resource material that is scanned is arranged alphabetically, such as a dictionary, the index of a book, a zip code directory and numerous reference listings.

Some material is not arranged alphabetically, such as the sports pages of the newspaper, television listings. We need to get familiar with the arrangement of information first and then proceed to find the section or page most likely to contain the information desired. Likewise, in order to answer a specific question or locate a specific bit of information in an article, we must become familiar with the arrangement of the material, taking a few minutes to read the title and subheads , looking at the illustrations, and reading the first and last paragraphs.

In scanning follow these steps:

1. Be sure to know what you want to find.
2. If you are not familiar with the material, find out its attainment, if necessary, skim and locate the section of the material that may contain the information you need.
3. Move your eyes very rapidly over the lines until you find the very information you want.

Follow-up Work   **Read the questions below first then scan the passage for the answers to the questions.**

. . . .

1. How did Cutrona carry out her studies of college students?

_____

2. What are the two key findings by Cutrona?

_____

3. What is Cutrona's conclusion based on her findings?

_____

College students whose parents always assured them they were able scholars earn higher grades than classmates with the same academic ability but less supportive parents, a new study suggests.

"Parents' attitudes toward their children seem to affect the way students think of themselves and self-image seems to influence performance," says psychologist Carolyn Cutrona of University of Iowa City.

Cutrona's studies of 797 students, mostly freshmen and sophomores, compared their college entrance exam scores to grade point averages. Students also filled out questionnaires on their families. Among key findings: students with the cheerleading parents showed less anxiety about challenges; lower anxiety was linked to more self-confidence, which predicted better grades.

Having supportive friends or romantic partners didn't affect grade point average. Few students were in daily contact with parents, says Cutrona, but findings "probably show a lifetime of being raised to have self-confidence".

Part E Banked Cloze

Direction: *In the following text, there are ten blanks. Read the text and then fill in each blank with a word from the word bank. Each choice in the bank is identified by a letter. Do not use any of the words more than twice.*

Computer File

A computer file is a block of arbitrary information, or resource for _____ (1) information, which is available to a computer program and is usually based on some kind of durable storage. A file is _____ (2) in the sense that it remains available for programs to use after the current program has finished. Computer files can be considered as the modern _____ (3) of paper documents which traditionally are kept in offices' and libraries' files, and this is the source of the term.

Information in a computer file can consist of smaller packets of information that are individually different but share some trait in common. For example, a payroll file might contain information _____ (4) all the employees in a company and their payroll details; each record in the payroll file concerns just one employee, and all the records have the common trait of being related to payroll — this is very similar to placing all payroll information into a specific filing _____ (5) in an office that does not have a computer. A text file may contain lines of text, corresponding to printed lines on a piece of paper.

The way information is grouped into a file is entirely up to how it is designed. Most computer files are used by computer _____ (6) which create, modify or delete the files for their own use on an as-needed basis. The programmers who create the programs decide what files are needed, how they are to be used and (often) their names.

In some _____ (7), computer programs manipulate files that are made visible to the computer user. For example, in a word-processing program, the user manipulates document files that the user personally names. Although the content of the document file is arranged in a format that the word-processing program understands, the user is able to choose the name and location of the _____ (8) and provide the bulk of the information (such as words and text) that will be stored in the file.

Many applications pack all their data files into a single file called _____ (9) file, using internal markers to discern the different types of information contained within. The benefits of the archive file are to lower the _____ (10) of files for easier transfer, to reduce storage usage, or just to organize outdated files. The archive file must often be unpacked before next using.

A) durable	B) cabinet	C) cases	D) concerning	E) archive
F) storing	G) number	H) file	I) counterpart	J) programs

Unit 4
Performance Management

Matrix

· **Team building**
· **Motivating**

Part A Brainstorming

Directions: *Read the following short story and then discuss the following questions.*

· ·

➢ *Who is stronger, the wind or the sun?*

➢ *While building a team, what ways would you take?*

The Wind and the Sun

The wind and the sun were disputing which was the stronger. Suddenly, they saw a traveler coming down the road, and the sun said, "I see a way to decide our dispute. Whichever of us can cause that traveler to take off his cloak shall be regarded as the stronger. You begin." So the sun retired behind a cloud, and the wind began to blow as hard as it could upon the traveler. But the harder he blew the more closely did the traveler wrap his cloak round him, till at last the wind had to give up in despair. Then the sun came out and shone in all his glory upon the traveler, who soon found it too hot to walk with his cloak on.

What can you get from the story?

A. Kindness effects more than severity.

B. Words speak louder than actions.

C. Words are weapons.

D. Self-conceit may lead to self-destruction.

Part B Team Building

Pre-reading Questions

➤ *How to keep employees interested in your message?*

➤ *Is there a one-size-fits-all approach for internal communication?*

A roundtable discussion on internal communications was recently held at a local public relations conference. Surprisingly, the most critical issue was on how to keep the rank and file employees interested in what the company had to say. For the most part, this seemed to be due to a lack of strategic thinking when it came to internal communications. If you are facing what you perceive to be sagging interest by your employees, here are a few questions you might ask yourself.

Do you know what actually interests your employees? Have you ever asked your employees what they want to know when you talk to them?

- First, employees need to hear things at three levels: the contextual, the strategic and the personal. At the first level, employees want to know, "What factors (external or internal) are causing the company to make the business decisions?" At the second level, an employee wants to know, "What are we doing to respond to those factors?" or "What's our strategy?" At the third level, they are asking, "What will all of this mean for me personally?"

- Second, employees want to hear the personal news directly from their manager. This means you need to help support management involvement in internal communications, which will make a good future topic.

Does your company understand why it's important for employees to be interested? Why is the personal level of communication so important? Why do so many senior managers have trouble making a time or financial commitment to internal communications? Perhaps it's because they don't understand that there is a solid business case for internal communications.

Last year, Towers Perrin, a New York-based human resources consulting firm, released a report on employee attitudes in the workplace. The report shows, for the most part, employees are miserable in their jobs, because they don't feel appreciated or connected to the overall mission of the company.

The connection here is really simple. In the United States, we tend to use jobs as a measure of our self-worth. When people don't see the relevance of their job in the overall scheme of things, they tend to feel badly about the company and they don't like their jobs as much.

However, in a second finding in this study — one that should awaken senior management — the study tracked a "statistically significant" correlation between positive employee emotions and companies' five-year shareholder return.

Recommended is a four-step process in improving your internal communication program that involves a coordinated effort between your top management, HR and communications department. It consists of training, accountability, rewards and support. This means: (1) train your managers to be communicators; (2) make your managers accountable for communication; (3) give them rewards and recognition for being good communicators; and (4) continually support them with talking points, suggestions and tips on how to make their communication better.

Do tactics direct your program or does strategy?

For argument's sake, let's say that senior management in the company is committed to a solid internal communications program. A common mistake companies make at this point is using a one-size-fits-all approach. Twenty years ago, the company newsletter was the panacea. Today, it's the intranet. The point is, there is no one aspect of your communications program that will be your silver bullet. It needs to encompass various aspects that work in tandem. For example: (1) Managers want to get information first, so they can be in front of any issues that may arise with employees. Some want reminders or "extra information" they can use to share information effectively. They may need remedial tips on communication and may need to have spelled out for them what employees are going to have questions about. (2) Some people just need the highlights and the name of the place they can go to get more information if they want it. Others want it all, all the time. Put communication in different places (e-mail, print, bulletin boards, etc.) to satisfy everyone's needs. Most people need to see or hear it multiple times, and in multiple ways, in order to understand the message completely. (3) Getting face time with a supervisor is important — it allows employees to ask questions. But, it's equally important they get something they can walk away with on paper. This gives them the opportunity to refer back to information once they've had time to absorb what they heard.

Task One Choose the best answer to fill in the blank.

. . . .

1. We have no interest in interfering in the _____ affairs of other countries.

    A．external   B．internal

    C．international   D．intentional

2. Even as a young woman she had been _____ as a future chief executive.

    A．perceived   B．received   C．deceived   D．conceived

3. The island is of _____ importance to China.

    A．logic   B．magic   C．strategy   D．strategic

4. Our company has a _____ to quality and customer service.

    A．apartment   B．commitment   C．compliment   D．development

5. Because of rising costs, the company _____ 10% of their workforce.

    A．relapsed   B．released   C．relaxed   D．related

6. The _____ cost of the exhibition was £400,000.

    A．overdue   B．overtime   C．overnight   D．overall

7. He owns a large company whose activities _____ printing, publishing and computers.

    A．encompass   B．enclose   C．encounter   D．entrust

8. The agencies are working together to _____ policy on food safety.

    A．cooperate   B．co-produce   C．coordinate   D．co-educate

Task Two Decide whether the following statements are true or false according to the text.

. . . .

1. (   ) The senior management of many companies doesn't have enough strategic thinking of internal communication.

2. (   ) There isn't much research on what actually interests employees across the country.

3. (   ) At the contextual level, employees wonder about the factors that lead the company to make decisions.

4. (   ) Many top managers haven't spent money and time on internal communications.

5. (   ) Employees will feel happy if they are more appreciated and related to the company.

Task Three   Translate the following sentences from the text into Chinese.

1. The most critical issue was on how to keep the rank and file employees interested in what the company had to say.

   _____

   _____

2. Employees need to hear things at three levels: the contextual, the strategic and the personal.

   _____

   _____

3. Why do so many senior managers have trouble making a time or financial commitment to internal communications?

   _____

   _____

4. The study tracked a "statistically significant" correlation between positive employee emotions and companies' five-year shareholder return.

   _____

   _____

5. A common mistake companies make at this point is using a one-size-fits-all approach.

   _____

   _____

Part C   Motivating

Pre-reading Questions

➢ *What is the relationship between motives, motivation and motivators?*
➢ *Are reward and punishment two motivators? Why?*

Human motives are based on needs, whether consciously or subconsciously felt. Some are primary needs, such as the physiological requirements for water, air, food, sleep, and shelter. Other needs may be regarded as secondary, such as self-esteem, status, affiliation with others, affection, giving, accomplishment, and self-assertion. Naturally, these needs vary in intensity and over time among different individuals.

Motivation is a general term applying to the entire class of drives, desires, needs, wishes, and similar forces. To say that managers motivate their subordinates is to say that they do those things which they hope will satisfy these drives and desires and induce the subordinates to act in a desired manner. Motivators are things that induce an individual to perform. While motivations reflect wants, motivators are the identified rewards, or incentives, that sharpen the drive to satisfy these wants. They are also the means by which conflicting needs may be reconciled or one need heightened so that it will be given priority over another.

A manager can do much to sharpen motives by establishing an environment favorable to certain drives. For example, people in a business that has developed a reputation for excellence and high quality tend to be motivated to contribute to this reputation. Similarly, the environment of a business in which managerial performance is effective and efficient tends to breed a desire for high-quality management among most, or all, managers and personnel.

A motivator, then, is something that influences an individual's behavior. It makes a difference in what a person will do. Obviously, in any organized enterprise, managers must be concerned about motivators and also inventive in their use. People can often satisfy their wants in a variety of ways. A person can, for example, satisfy a desire for affiliation by being active in a social club rather than in a business, meet economic needs by performing a job just well enough to get by, or satisfy status needs by spending time working for a political party. What a manager must do, of course, is to use those motivators which will lead people to perform effectively for the enterprise that employs them.

Motivation refers to the drive and effort to satisfy a want or goal. Satisfaction refers to the contentment experienced when a want is satisfied. In other words, motivation implies a drive toward an outcome, and satisfaction is the outcome already experienced.

From a management point of view, then, a person might have high job satisfaction but a low level of motivation for the job, or the reverse might be true. Understandably, the probability exists that highly motivated persons with low job satisfaction will look for other positions. Likewise, people who find their positions rewarding but are being paid considerably less than they desire or think they deserve will probably search for other jobs.

The various leading theories of motivation and motivators seldom make reference to the carrot and the stick. This metaphor relates, of course, to the use of rewards and penalties in order to induce desired behavior. It comes from the old story that to make a donkey move, one must put a carrot in front of him or jab him with a stick from behind.

Despite all the research on and theories of motivation that have come to the fore in recent years, reward and punishment are still considered strong motivators. For centuries, however, they were too often thought of as the only forces that could motivate people. In fact, there are many other motivators.

At the same time, in all theories of motivation, the inducements of some kinds of "carrot" are recognized. Often the "carrot" is money in the form of pay or bonuses. Even though money is not the only motivating force, it has been and will continue to be an important one. The trouble with the money "carrot" approach is that too often everyone gets a carrot, regardless of performance, through such practices as salary increases and promotion by seniority, automatic "merit" increases, and executive bonuses not based on individual manager performance.

The "stick," in the form of fear — fear of loss of job, loss of income, reduction of bonus, demotion, or some other penalty — has been and continues to be a strong motivator. Yet it is admittedly not the best kind. It often gives rise to defensive or retaliatory behavior, such as union organization, poor-quality work, executive indifference, failure of a manager to take any risks in decision making, or even dishonesty. But fear of penalty cannot be overlooked. Whether managers are first-level supervisors or chief executives, the power of their position to give or withhold rewards or impose penalties of various kinds gives them an ability to control, to a very great extent, the economic and social wellbeing of their subordinates. It is hardly a wonder that many subordinates are "yes-sayers", simply agreeing with their superiors rather than using their considered judgment.

Task One Fill in the blanks with the expressions given below. Change the form when necessary.

. . . .

> primary; motivate; incentive; tension; induce; retaliatory; challenge; portray; self-esteem; merit

1. The diary _____ his family as quarrelsome and malicious.

2. The _____ reason for advertising is to sell more goods.

3. They don't try very hard, but then there's no _____.

4. Making one's own decisions increases a child's sense of control and boosts his/her _____.

5. I've found that the best way to _____ them is to let them know the game plan so they can all be part of it.

6. There's been talk of a(n) _____ blockade to prevent supplies getting through.

7. There's no _____ in giving away what you don't really want.

8. Reducing the gap between the rich and the poor is one of the main _____ facing the government.

9. She had at first hoped to _____ Mr. Woodhouse to remove with her to Donwell.

10. The incident has further increased the _____ between the two countries.

Task Two Choose the best answer according to the passage.

1. This passage mainly talks about _____.

   A. motivators which are things that induce an individual to perform

   B. motivation which refers to the drive and effort to satisfy a want or goal

   C. various leading theories of motivation and motivators

   D. the "carrot and stick" metaphor which comes from an old story that is to make a donkey move

2. According to the passage, which of the following is NOT the primary need of human motives?

   A. Bread.   B. Fresh water.   C. Apartment.   D. Love.

3. The word "subordinate" means _____.

   A. someone who has a lower position and less authority

   B. someone who has a higher position and more authority

   C. someone who has a lower position but more authority

   D. someone who has a higher position but less authority

4. According to the passage, which of the following statements is TRUE?

   A. Motivations are things that induce a person to perform.

   B. People can often satisfy their wants in a variety of ways.

   C. Reward and punishment are not considered strong motivators.

   D. The money "carrot" is the only motivating force.

5. A "yes-sayer" is the person who _____.

   A. uses their considered judgment   B. agrees with his/her superiors simply

C. takes risks in decision making   D. fears loss of job and income

Task Three **Sum up the main idea of the text in 100 words.**

_____

_____

_____

_____

Part D Reading Strategy

Choosing Reading Speeds

Reading speeds vary with people and the material they read. However, we can talk about three levels of speed: slow, normal and fast.

We use different speeds for different purposes. Choosing a reading speed or reading rate is picking the right reading speed. Reading flexibility is another term for choosing the right reading speed.

Some material is very easy to read, and some, rather hard to read. The readability of the material is how hard or easy it is to read. Hard material has low readability. Easy material has high readability. For example: a passage is harder, and thus less readable, if it has hard words; if it has no headings or topic sentences; if the topic (main idea) is not stated in the first sentence of the paragraph; if the sentences are long and complex; and so on. Ont the other hand, a passage is easier, and thus more readable, if it has easy words; if it has headings and topic sentences; if the topic is stated in the first sentence of the paragraph; if the sentences are short and simple; and so on.

Our readiness to read is based on two things: what we already know about the content (the topic) of the material and how well we can use the reading skills.

We choose a slow speed when our purpose calls for 100% understanding, when the material has a low level of readability or our readiness to read the material is low.

We choose a normal speed when our purpose calls for a high level of understanding, but not 100% understanding, when the material is fairly readable, or our readiness for reading the material is fairly good.

We use a fast speed when our purpose does not call for 100% understanding, when the material is very readable, and when our readiness for reading the material is high.

Here are steps to choose a reading speed:

➢ Set your goal for reading. Choosing the level of understanding you need to reach.

➢ Preview the material very carefully. Pay very close attention to questions that help you decide about the readability of the material and your readiness to read the material. Be sure to look at the technical vocabulary to see whether you should study it before you start to read.

➢ Choose the speed you are going to try for. Put together your goal and what you have learned from previewing. And choose the speed that you think is best: slow, normal or fast.

➢ Read the material at the speed you have chosen and find your level of understanding.

➢ Make adjustments if necessary. Reread the material if your level of understanding was lower than the level you set as your goal. Make yourself go faster next time if your level of understanding was good but your wpm was lower than you wished.

Follow-up Work **Read the following passages and mark "Right", "Wrong" or "Doesn't say". Record the time you have used and the number of correct answers you have got.**

Passage 1

Time _____ Score _____

How to Move Office

A successful office relocation demands careful preparation. It's important to form a project team as early as possible before the move, and at least twelve months in advance. It's also essential to contact the British Association of Removers and ask for a list of commercial specialists who will advise on packing, security and other important topics. Internally you'll need to appoint a move organizer, or employ a freelance expert from a firm such as Move Plan, which organizes relocation for firms from two to 6,000 people. You'll also need to pick a time when closing down your IT department will cause the fewest problems to the business and, for that reason, the majority of firms now move over a weekend. Next make a list of all the furniture, equipment and paperwork. Commercial movers will pack filing in A－Z order, so if A－G leaves the building, it's still A－G when it's unpacked. Confidential files can be sealed in secure boxes for moving day. Commercial specialists will keep company employees fully informed and answer any questions they may have. You may move offices once or twice in your career, but experts do it every year.

1. According to the article, the minimum planning time for an office move should be a year.

   A. Right   B. Wrong   C. Doesn't say.

2. The writer says that companies should be able to organize their move without external help.

   A. Right   B. Wrong   C. Doesn't say.

3. Move Plan is a company good at organizing both large and small moves.

   A. Right   B. Wrong   C. Doesn't say.

4. The IT department is usually the first department to move.

   A. Right   B. Wrong   C. Doesn't say.

5. Most companies believe there are fewer computer problems if the move happens Monday to Friday.

   A. Right   B. Wrong   C. Doesn't say.

6. Companies are advised to pack confidential materials themselves.

   A. Right   B. Wrong   C. Doesn't say.

7. A specialist remover will make sure stuff is kept up to date with arrangements for its move.

   A. Right   B. Wrong   C. Doesn't say.

8. A successful office relocation demands careful preparation.

   A. Right   B. Wrong   C. Doesn't say.

Passage 2

Time _____ Score _____

Zurich's Hotel for Women Only

Business travel can be difficult for everyone, but especially for women. Traveling alone in a strange city, women often don't want to go out at night and visit local attractions themselves. Dining alone at a restaurant can be depressing. Many women spend the evening in their hotel rooms — using room service, watching television and eating snacks from the mini-bar. Life is not always so exciting for a traveling businesswoman. That's why a new hotel in Zurich, Switzerland, offers an interesting alternative for women business travelers — a "women-only" hotel. The Lady's First Hotel and its Wellness Center opened in January, 2001. Men aren't allowed in, and all the staffs are female. The hotel was designed by architect Pia Schmid, with women business travelers in mind. It is a small hotel with 28 rooms. Guests can meet in the lobby, and sit around a fireplace. Light refreshments are available in the hotel bar and mini-bar snacks include healthy food, not only chocolate and alcohol. Bathrooms are well-lit and have extra amenities. Meeting and conference rooms are available. The best aspect of Lady's First is the Wellness Center. The facilities are located on the top floor of the hotel and offer a wide variety of health and beauty treatments. The Wellness Center has a steam room, saunas and a terrace overlooking the lake and mountains.

1. Women traveling alone often prefer to stay in their hotel rooms.

   A. Right   B. Wrong   C. Doesn't say.

2. The hotel only employs women.

   A. Right   B. Wrong   C. Doesn't say.

3. There isn't any chocolate or alcohol in the mini-bar.

   A. Right   B. Wrong   C. Doesn't say.

4. There aren't any meeting rooms.

   A. Right   B. Wrong   C. Doesn't say.

5. The Wellness Center is near reception.

   A. Right   B. Wrong   C. Doesn't say.

6. You have a beautiful view from the Wellness Center.

    A. Right   B. Wrong   C. Doesn't say.

7. The facilities in the bathrooms are excellent.

    A. Right   B. Wrong   C. Doesn't say.

8. Business travel can be difficult for everyone, but especially for women.

    A. Right   B. Wrong   C. Doesn't say.

Part E   Banked Cloze

Direction: *In the following text, there are ten blanks. Read the text and then fill in each blank with a word from the word bank. Each choice in the bank is identified by a letter. Do not use any of the words more than twice.*

Team Building Essentials

Team building skills are _____ (1) for your effectiveness as a manager or an entrepreneur. And even if you are not in a management or leadership role yet, better understanding of team work can make you a more _____ (2) employee and give you an extra edge in your corporate office.

A team building success is when your team can _____ (3) something much bigger and work more effectively than a group of the same individuals working on their own.

Here are some additional team building ideas, techniques, and tips you can _____ (4) when managing teams in your situation.

- Make sure that the team goals are totally clear and _____ (5) understood and accepted by each team member.

- Make sure there is complete clarity in who is _____ (6) for what and avoid overlapping authority.

- Build trust with your team members by spending one-on-one time in a(n) _____ (7) of honesty and openness. Be loyal to your employees, if you expect the same.

- Allow your office team members build trust and openness between each other in team building activities and events. Give them some opportunities of extra social time with each other in an atmosphere that _____ (8) open communication.

- For issues that rely heavily on the team consensus and commitment, try to _____ (9) the whole team in the decision making process.

- When managing teams, make sure there are no blocked lines of communications and you and your people are _____ (10) fully informed.

A) try	B) completely	C) critical	D) kept	E) atmosphere
F) involve	G) accomplish	H) encourages	I) responsible	J) effective

Unit 5
Conference Management

Matrix

· **Attending a conference**
· **Organizing a conference**

Part A Brainstorming

Directions: *Read the following short story and fill in the blank. And then discuss the following questions.*

➢ *What was the CEO going to do?*
➢ *What can you learn from the funny story?*

Two Copies

A young blonde executive was leaving the office one evening when she noticed the CEO standing in front of the shredder with a piece of paper in his hand.

"Listen," said the CEO, "this is important, and my assistant has left for the day. Can you make this thing work?"

"Certainly," she turned the machine on, inserted the paper, and pressed the START button before the CEO said the following words:

"I hope you _____."

The following information may do help to expand your thinking perspective:

1. Why does the executive think the CEO wants to shred the paper?
2. In fact, what does the CEO want to do?
3. However, what did the executive do?

Part B Attending a Negotiation

Pre-reading Questions

➢ *How do you reach an agreement in a negotiation?*

➢ *How can you make an offer that aims at the other party's most important need?*

It happens time and again during a negotiating session, as the discussion begins and the two sides face each other across the conference room table. Party One: "I'll give you one and a half million dollars for this building and not a penny more." Party Two: "It's worth at least twice that. I wouldn't sell it for a dime less than one million eight hundred thousand."

You have seen or done this type of horse-trading and, frankly, there are no fancy ways of making it work better than the back and forth threatening and cajoling you already know. But this is not the usual real world deal. And there is a better way. What is different about the real world is that, typically, the deal has many more dimensions than just price. As an example, even buying frozen peas may be more complex than a building sale. Do you want eight ounces or 16? A box or a bag? You probably won't dicker over one bag, but what if you were buying for a large social supper and need 20 pounds? Would you try to get a better price? And if you wanted to buy that building, would you try to get a better price by offering a certified check next Tuesday, so the seller does not have to wait for a loan to be approved for you?

The deal has just become "multi-dimensional", as are most deals. How can it be successfully negotiated? The way most people negotiate is based on taking a position and then making concessions from it. Obviously, many deals have been done that way from the beginning of commerce 10 thousand years ago and maybe earlier. But there is an alternative process, one that can get to a conclusion faster and with less friction, and that's needs-based bargaining.

Here's how it works. How do you know what concession to make to get closer to a deal? By guessing? Should you, as the seller, simply drop the price for your goods? How do you know what is most important for the buyer? What would happen if you just asked the buyer what's important to him? Would he answer? Most smart buyers will not tell you the absolute top price they would pay for your goods without walking away from the deal. That, after all, is the key piece of information they are holding back. If you knew it, you might just offer to sell at that price, even if you would make money at a lower price. But the top price to buy is not the question you ask. Instead, you ask what the important factors are for the person on the other side, without asking to discuss specifics, or "parameters". Then, you ask questions to prioritize those factors. Eventually, you aim to come out to see, in multiple dimensions, how he sees what he needs. He is not sure, if he does not know you, what use you might make of the information. Trust is not yet established. What can you do about that problem? Why not reveal what your needs are? After all, you are the one trying to use needs-based negotiation. Say, "What is most important to me in this deal is actually not this one sale to you, but doing a series of them over the next year. At the same time, my company is not in a position to extend more than a modest period of credit on each sale." Your revealing some information will likely increase the amount of trust the other side has in you. In response, he will likely open up some as well. After all, telling you his needs will actually enable you to put together a proposal or offer that will at least come closer more quickly to what he needs than beating around the bush.

It may take several times around the dance floor for both sides to exchange a complete list of their needs, and you should stay with the process until both do. Neither may have thought of everything the first time, and neither may be comfortable right off with this somewhat unusual process. You may have to remind the other side, and yourself, that you are not asking what his position is, but what in principle his needs are. If after a few rounds he is still not forthcoming, he may not really be ready to deal, and you should back away.

Needs-based negotiation has been taught and refined over more than 25 years, among other places at the Harvard Negotiation Project, and is an effective method. Try it soon. You may like the results.

Task One Choose the best answer to fill in the blank.

. . . .

1. Both sides still refuse to come to the _____ table.

   A. negotiation   B. communication   C. communicate   D. connection

2. The boss's promise to increase the workers' pay was a _____ to union demands.

   A. confession   B. concession   C. session   D. accession

3. The Minister _____ a commission to suggest improvement in the educational system.

 A．built B．set C．established D．settled

4. The investigation has _____ some serious faults in the system.

 A．referred B．revealed C．released D．relieved

5. A chamber of _____ is an organization of businessmen that promotes local commercial

 interests.

 A．comment B．commence C．commission D．commerce

6. The _____ that the hospital should be closed was rejected by a large majority.

 A．problem B．property C．proposal D．proverb

7. He couldn't block the deal unless _____ buyers existed.

 A．alterable B．alternative C．always D．altogether

8. The equipment must be bought from a supplier _____ by the company.

 A．proved B．approved C．applied D．apologized

Task Two Decide whether the following statements are true or false according to the text.

. . . .

1. (   ) The two parties in the negotiation should focus on nothing but the price.

2. (   ) The buyer would buy a building at a lower price if he offered the seller a certified check.

3. (   ) People usually provide a price and then make concessions from it when making a deal.

4. (   ) The needs-based bargaining can make the negotiation faster and smoother.

5. (   ) Few buyers will let you know their top price during the negotiation because it is critical

 information.

Task Three Translate the following sentences from the text into Chinese.

. . . .

1. You have seen or done this type of horse-trading and，frankly，there are no fancy ways of making

 it work better than the back and forth threatening and cajoling you already know.

 _____

 _____

2. But there is an alternative process, one that can get to a conclusion faster and with less friction, and that's needs-based bargaining.

_____

_____

3. Most smart buyers will not tell you the absolute top price they would pay for your goods without walking away from the deal.

_____

_____

4. What is most important to me in this deal is actually not this one sale to you, but doing a series of them over the next year.

_____

_____

5. After all, telling you his needs will actually enable you to put together a proposal or offer that will at least come closer more quickly to what he needs than beating around the bush.

_____

_____

Part C Organizing a Conference

Pre-reading Questions

➢ *What is a secretary supposed to do before the conference?*

➢ *What is a secretary supposed to do during the conference?*

Before the Conference

1. *Define the purpose of the conference*

Before making any arrangements, the secretary must consult the boss or the conference organizing committee (if the conference is a large one) to reach the final decisions on main theme or purpose of the conference and the date and the place.

2. *Develop an agenda in cooperation with key participants*

Some days before the conference is to take place, your boss will have given you the items he wishes to put on the agenda and told you who else to ask for other items. You will either present a draft of the agenda to your boss for his revision, or once you are established in your job and he feels it appropriate, he will leave the entire preparation to you. Make sure you note on the agenda the people concerned with each item and any papers attached or previously circulated. In pencil on the chairman's agenda, note anything he particularly wants to raise and discuss. Afterwards, distribute the agenda and circulate background material, lengthy documents or articles prior to the conference so that all members will be prepared and feel involved and up-to-date.

3. *Choose a location suitable to your group's size*

Small rooms with too many people get stuffy and create tension. A larger room is more comfortable and encourages individual expression. If possible, arrange the room so that members face each other, i. e., a circle or semi-circle. For large groups, try U-shaped rows. If it is a fairly large conference, the secretary and the organizing committee must go to a hotel to book accommodation and entertainment for the attendants, and calculate all the cost. The conference room must be appropriately equipped with all the devices or equipment having to be used during the conference. If there are other activities prior to, in the middle of, and after the conference, such as conference dinner, reception, a trip, etc., careful arrangements should be made for them. What's more, the secretary should contact the press and invite some reporters and photographers if the conference needs publicity, and make further arrangements for them, including certain facilities and equipment. Sometimes use visual aids for interest (e. g. posters, diagrams, etc.).

4. *Take necessary conference files*

The secretary will take with her the Minute Book containing the agreed minutes of previous conferences, previously circulated papers, an attendance register to be signed by all those attending the conference and a shorthand notebook. Besides, post a large agenda up front to which members can refer just in case any member has neglected to bring his own.

During the Conference

1. *Create a relaxing atmosphere*

Secretaries can greet members and make them feel welcomed, even late members when appropriate. If possible, serve light refreshments; they are good icebreakers and make your members feel special and comfortable.

2. *Encourage group discussion to get all points of view and ideas*

With a good chairman, a conference will proceed through the agenda efficiently, with enough time being allowed for the various items to be discussed, members of the conference being tactfully kept to the subject and action indicated before moving on to the next item. With better quality decisions, the highly motivated members will feel that attending conferences is worthy. Meanwhile, keep conversation focused on the topic and ask for only constructive and non-repetitive comments. Tactfully end discussions when attendants are getting nowhere or becoming destructive or unproductive.

3. *Keep minutes of the conference for future reference in case a question or problem arises*

At conferences, the secretary's major task is just to take notes and record the details of the decisions or arrangements reached. However, there are a number of points to bear in mind. The minutes of a conference are not a verbatim record. A two-hour conference may well produce only one A4 sheet of minutes. Be brief, but be sure she does not miss any items of importance and decision. A secretary must remember that she is a part of the conference only in her capacity as a record keeper. She is not required to comment directly on the conference in any way whatsoever. She can speak only when directly addressed, and this will probably be on a matter of checking dates or referring to past papers or reading back an item previously minuted. It can be difficult for a secretary to remain silent in some conferences, but in formal conferences this is not an absolute rule, but even so, she should wait until she is asked for an opinion before giving it. If a secretary always writes the minutes for particular conferences, she will soon become adjusted to the pattern they follow and will be able to make sense of what at first may appear to be in a total jumble of information.

After the Conference

When the conference is over, it is preferable for the secretary to write up and distribute minutes as soon as possible. Quick action reinforces importance of conference and reduces errors of memory. It is advisable for a secretary to type a first draft for her own revision, a second draft for her boss's comments and revision and finally a fair copy for duplication and circulation to the members of the conference and others who need to be informed. The sooner after a conference the minutes are received, the sooner the members are reminded of things they have undertaken to do. If necessary, write a report of the conference for issue to the attendants and possibly for the press.

Task One Fill in the blanks with the words given below. Change the form when necessary.

---

define ; agenda ; circulate ; distribute ; refreshment ; destructive ; capacity ; duplicate ; press ; advisable

1. What is the next item on the _____ ?
2. _____ are drinks and small amounts of food that are provided, for example, during a meeting or a journey.
3. This research merely _____ work already done elsewhere.
4. Because of the popularity of the region, it is _____ to book hotels or camp sites in advance.
5. The mountain was sharply _____ against the eastern sky.
6. Have you been _____ with details of the conference?
7. Children are generally _____ ; they like breaking things.
8. When a company _____ goods, it supplies them to the shops or businesses that sell them.
9. The majority of the _____ support the Government's foreign policy.
10. Some people have a greater _____ for happiness than others.

Task Two Choose the best answer according to the passage.

1. What is a secretary supposed to do before a conference?
    A. Define the purpose of the conference.
    B. Develop an agenda in cooperation with key participants.
    C. Choose a location suitable to your group's size.
    D. All of the above.
2. What kind of conference room is preferred?
    A. A small room, if possible.
    B. A room big enough to hold the conference.
    C. A large room equipped with all the devices.

D. Being cheap is the most important aspect.

3. What files should the secretary take with her when attending a conference?

    A. The Minute Book.   B. An attendance register.

    C. A shorthand notebook.   D. All of the above.

4. What is the secretary's major task at a meeting?

    A. Creating a serious atmosphere.

    B. Encouraging group discussion to get all points of view and ideas.

    C. Keeping minutes of the meeting for future reference in case a question or problem arises.

    D. Giving some services to meet the needs.

5. How should a secretary keep minutes of a meeting?

    A. The minutes of a meeting are a verbatim record.

    B. The minutes should be as brief as possible.

    C. When wanting to say something, a secretary should wait until being asked.

    D. A secretary can comment directly on the meeting.

Task Three **Sum up the main idea of the text in 100 words.**

_____

_____

_____

_____

Part D Reading Strategy

Guessing Word Meanings Through Context Clues

Context clues are the words surrounding the unfamiliar word which provide clues to the word's meaning. The followings are some types of context clues.

Definition

means, to be, refer to, be called, be defined as, be termed as, punctuation such as dashes, parenthesis and commas, etc.

 e.g. This is a <u>drawback</u>, a disadvantage, to that suggestion.

   (drawback＝disadvantage)

Apposition

 e.g. Mrs. White was surprised to see me in her office. She gave me a <u>startled</u> look, then smiled and asked, "What are you doing here?"

   (startled＝surprised)

Example

like, especially, include, special, consist of, for example, for instance, such as, ect.

Newly married couples often spend their money on home <u>appliances</u>, for example, TVs, air conditioners and refrigerators.

 (appliance＝a piece of equipment, especially electrical equipment)

Synonym

or, and, also, meaning, moreover, besides, further, likewise, similarly, in addition, as well as, the same as, etc.

 e.g. Experts believe that drinking is detrimental to our health. Similarly, they also consider smoking cigarettes harmful.

   (detrimental＝harmful)

Antonym

But, yet, however, while, whereas, unlike, otherwise, despite, in contrast, compared to, on the other hand, on the contrary, as opposed to, to the opposite, in spite of, even though, etc.

 e.g. Years ago, the world seemed to run in an orderly way. But now, everything appears to be in a state of <u>turmoil</u>.

   (turmoil＝disorder)

Restatement

or, that is, i.e., to be precise, in other words, to put it another way, that is to say, etc.

e.g.　People in big cities are used to spending hours in <u>gridlock</u>, that is, traffic so terrible that it simply doesn't move.

(gridlock＝traffic so terrible that it simply doesn't move)

Common sense

e.g.　Rubber can be made to extend eight times its normal length because it is quite <u>elastic</u>.

(elastic＝flexible)

Cause and effect

because, since, as, for, thus, so, hence, therefore, consequently, accordingly, due to, now that, seeing that, result in, result from, as a result, so … that, such … that, so that, for this (that) reason, etc.

e.g.　Since I could not afford the original painting, I purchased a <u>replica</u> instead. An inexperienced person could not tell the difference.

(replica＝a false or not real object)

Logical relationship

e.g.　If you are able to work eight hours a day without a rest, or if you can do physical exercise for hours without seeming to get tired, then you are a person who is <u>indefatigable</u>.

(indefatigable＝not easily tired)

Follow-up Work **Try to figure out the meanings of the underlined words as well as the context clue types you make use of. Then write your answers in the corresponding blanks.**

· ·

1. A good manger can easily tell the <u>adept</u> employees from the unskilled ones.

adept ＝ 　　　　　　　　context clue type：

2. If you agree, nod your head; if you <u>dissent</u>, shake your head.

dissent ＝ 　　　　　　　　context clue type：

3. Select a <u>periodical</u> from among the following: *Times*, *Fortune*, *Newsweek*, *The New Yorker* and *The Economist*.

   periodical =   context clue type:

4. It is impolite to insult and <u>defame</u> the person just because you disagree with him or her.

   defame =   context clue type:

5. The young man found himself in a tough situation, to be precise, his <u>plight</u> was so serious that he decided to ask for help from his friends.

   plight =   context clue type:

6. Jim's four-year-old nephew likes to fight for his <u>autonomy</u> by saying "I can do it myself".

   Autonomy =   context clue type:

7. Tom was so <u>exhausted</u> since he had overworked for days without enough rest.

   exhausted =   context clue type:

8. A group of <u>entrepreneurs</u> — people who own and run their own small business — attended that meeting.

   entrepreneurs =   context clue type:

9. Jeff felt quite <u>perturbed</u>, to put it another way, he was greatly disturbed by his roommates' actions.

   perturbed =   context clue type:

10. She often seemed to be involved in helpful activities rather than <u>destructive</u> ones.

    destructive =   context clue type:

Part E Banked Cloze

Direction: *In the following text, there are ten blanks. Read the text and then fill in each blank with a word from the word bank. Each choice in the bank is identified by a letter. Do not use any of the words more than twice.*

Confidence Is Everything

A business meeting is formal, _____ (1) when it is a meeting between people from separate companies. Formal introductions and _____ (2) of business cards are usually done at the start of the meeting. The organizer keeps the _____ (3) of the meeting and makes the meeting as efficient as possible.

Attending on international conference is a big event. There are a number of things to take care when attending. We will try to highlight some of the items for _____ (4) conferences. When attending an international conference, you are attending as a scholar or a businessman. Confidence is everything. To be confident, you _____ (5) prepare well.

Presentation is a skill that did not receive much attention in the Chinese universities. In the United States, almost _____ (6) Department of Humanities in the universities offers Public Speaking class. Most people need to be trained for this skill.

When you first _____ (7) to the stage for presentation, take a deep breath, and start talking when you are ready. Do not be scared by the eyes of the audience. Make eye contacts _____ (8) them. Use your gesture and high and low tones of voice. Make sure the microphone works before you start talking. If you can hear your voice quite loud, you feel you have _____ (9) and control of the presentation, which makes you confident. Don't be afraid that you repeated something. To get your ideas _____ (10), there are at least three things that you repeat three times in a presentation.

A) come	B) exchange	C) every	D) attending	E) across
F) pace	G) should	H) with	I) power	J) especially

Unit 6
Business Trip Management

Matrix

- **Planning a business trip**
- **Arranging travel and accommodations**

Part A Brainstorming

Directions: *Read the following short story and fill in the blank. And then discuss the following questions.*

. . . .

➢ *What happened to my colleague?*
➢ *What can you learn from the story?*

On a business trip to India, a colleague of mine arrived at the airport in Delhi. He took a taxi to his hotel, where he was greeted by his hospitable Indian host. The cab driver requested the equivalent of eight U.S. dollars for the fare, which seemed reasonable, so my friend handed him the money. But the host grabbed the bills and initiated a verbal assault upon the cabby, calling him a worthless parasite and a disgrace to their country for trying to overcharge visitors. The host threw half the amount at the driver and told him never to return. As the taxi sped off, the host gave the remaining bills to my colleague and asked him how his trip had been. "Fine," the business-man replied, "until you chased the cab away _____."

The following information may do help to expand your thinking perspective:

1. My colleague has got half of the money back, and he should be happy, but he is not. Why?
2. What is my colleague most unhappy with, the taxi driver's behavior or the host's overreaction or something else?

Part B Planning a Business Trip

Pre-reading Questions

➢ *How to plan a business trip?*

➢ *What are the factors to consider in making travel arrangements?*

When you plan a business trip, you can search for the best route online, and make travel arrangements that are both cost effective and comfortable. And it's not just the actual flight you can book — you can also pre-book accommodation, offsite airport parking, rental cars and sightseeing trips.

Fly direct if you can, but if you can't, then leave some flexibility in the schedule. This is good both for missed connections and for your own health. Making your connection a couple of hours later than your inward flight will free you from a possible five-mile-jog across an airport with your luggage. You need to choose a reliable airline. Many sites offer data on which airlines experience fewest delays. This could make your journey much more pleasant. If you are a frequent flyer, then pick an airline that serves most of your regular destinations and join the frequent flyer program. That will give you lots of travel perks, and it works for airlines, car hire and parking too.

If you're on a short trip, travel light with just a laptop and a carry-on. This will cut down on security checks and make it quicker to leave the airport at your destination. If you are on a longer trip, keep important documents with you (you can print them out ahead of time) so you won't have to worry about messing up an important presentation if your luggage goes missing or gets damaged. You can also use travel time to study any important notes or documents before your meeting.

Technology is your friend. With a good cell phone, pager, laptop or any combination of the three, you don't need to leave the rest of your work behind when you're on a business trip. You can keep tabs on the latest information and handle urgent situations while heading to your next destination. You should allow for some down time. If you're lucky, your company is flexible about the fact that you're traveling on your own time. Leave some time to relax and have fun. It will help you be a more effective business person and will protect your health too.

Finally, if you are a regular traveler, make a checklist for everything you need to accomplish before you travel and print it out before your next trip. This will streamline your travel arrangements and remove even more of the stress from your business trip.

Task One Choose the best answer to fill in the blank.

. . . .

1. We stopped at Paris en _____ from Rome to London.

   A. rout   B. route   C. routine   D. routing

2. The council should be able to help families who have no _____.

   A. accommodate   B. accommodation

   C. accommodating   D. accommodated

3. You have considerable _____ in this job and can choose how to do things.

   A. flexible   B. flex   C. flexing   D. flexibility

4. One of the _____ of being a student is cheap travel.

   A. perks   B. pars   C. parks   D. pores

5. It is the _____ of wit and political analysis that makes his articles so readable.

   A. comb   B. combining

   C. combination   D. combustion

6. A stupid medical clerk had slipped the wrong _____ on his X-ray.

   A. tab   B. tap   C. tad   D. tag

7. We greatly overestimate what we can _____ in one year. But we greatly underestimate what we can _____ in ten years.

   A. accomplishment   B. accommodate

   C. accompany   D. accomplish

8. He is determined on his new plans to _____ the company and make it more profitable and competitive.

   A. stream   B. streamline

   C. steam   D. esteem

Task Two   Decide whether the following statements are true or false according to the text.

. . . .

1. (   ) You can pre-book rental cars when you plan a business trip.
2. (   ) Leave some flexibility in your schedule if you can't fly direct.
3. (   ) Joining the frequent flyer program could make your journey much more pleasant.
4. (   ) Travel perks work for airlines, car hire and sightseeing trips.
5. (   ) Keeping important documents with you will cut down on security checks and make it quicker to leave the airport at your destination.

Task Three   Translate the following sentences from the text into Chinese.

. . . .

1. When you plan a business trip, you can search for the best route online, and make travel arrangements that are both cost effective and comfortable.

_____

_____

2. Making your connection a couple of hours later than your inward flight will free you from a possible five-mile-jog across an airport with your luggage.

_____

_____

3. If you are a frequent flyer, then pick an airline that serves most of your regular destinations and join the frequent flyer program.

_____

_____

4. If you're on a short trip, travel light with just a laptop and a carry-on.

_____

_____

5. This will streamline your travel arrangements and remove even more of the stress from your business trip.

_____

Part C Arranging Travel and Accommodations

Pre-reading Questions

➤ *How to choose your mode of transportation?*

➤ *How to make your reservations?*

Arranging travel can be a daunting task, especially if you have never done it. It involves making preparations to get to your destination of choice, where to stay when you get there, and what to do once you're there. Not sure how to begin? A good starting point is deciding where you'd like to go, and how much you'd like to spend.

1. Decide on a destination. Which state or country would you like to visit? Do you want to travel to a warm climate or a cold climate? Do you like seeing historical sights, walking through museums, lying on a sunny beach, trying your luck in a casino, getting a thrill at an amusement park, walking or hiking beautiful landscapes ... The choices are endless, but they can only be made by you.

2. Decide when you want to travel. Do you want to travel during winter, spring, summer or fall? Destinations, such as Las Vegas and Miami can be more expensive to visit during the winter months. Conversely, a trip to Disney World in early January can be the most economical time to visit the amusement park. If you want to keep your travel costs low, consider your time of travel carefully.

3. Choose your mode of transportation. Will you drive, fly or ride the train to your destination. Consider the total costs of transportation. Does your rental car have fees for going over the mileage? Does the airline assess baggage charges? Is driving to your destination faster than taking the train? How much will you spend on gas? Check fares on-line to get an idea of your travel costs and decide if it falls within your budget.

4. Choose a hotel. What type of hotel do you prefer, budget or four-star? How many rooms will you need? Do you need a non-smoking room? Again, there are countless travel websites to assist you in making these choices. Orbitz.com, Expedia.com and Hotels.com are three popular

choices, but there are many more. Use these sites to check availability and compare rates.

5. Make your reservations. Once you decide on where and when you'd like to go, how you'll get there and where you'll stay, book your arrangements, either on-line or by phone. Be careful when making airline or train reservations. Many of the low-cost options are non-refundable, so if you're after the best price, be sure you'll actually be able to go on the dates and times you choose. Hotel reservations are usually more flexible with their cancellation policies, however many offer "Web-only" rates that may be non-refundable. Make sure you know what you're buying before actually buying it.

Task One Fill in the blanks with the expressions given below. Change the form when necessary.

> daunt; thrill; historical; amusement; converse; assess; budget; countless; refundable;
> cancellation

1. There are _____ small ski areas dotted about the province.
2. "He is happy but not rich" is the _____ of "He is rich but not happy".
3. The prospect of meeting the President is quite _____ .
4. It would be a matter of _____ whether she was well enough to travel.
5. The children were _____ to bits by their presents.
6. We may be able to offer you some tickets if we have any _____ .
7. He stopped and watched with _____ to see the child so absorbed.
8. If we _____ carefully, we'll be able to afford a new car.
9. He is writing a _____ novel about the nineteenth-century France.
10. We will require a _____ deposit of 500 RMB to guarantee the airfare.

Task Two Choose the best answer according to the Passage.

1. What does the passage mainly talk about?

A . Deciding when and where you want to travel.

B . Choosing your mode of transportation.

C . Ways to choose your hotel and make your reservations.

D . All of the above.

2. According to the passage, when is the most economical time to visit Disney World?

A . January.

B . April.

C . September.

D . November.

3. According to the passage, which of the following websites is NOT recommended to check availability and compare rates?

A . Orbitz.com.

B . Expedia.com.

C . Hostel.com.

D . Hotels.com.

4. According to the passage, which of the following statements is TRUE?

A . Las Vegas and Miami can be more expensive to visit during the summer months.

B . Many of the low-cost options are refundable when making airline or train reservations.

C . Hotel reservations are usually more flexible with their cancellation policies.

D . "Web-only" means the reservation rate is non-refundable.

5. According to the passage, the total costs of transportation include _____ .

A . Flight tickets

B . Train tickets and baggage charges

C . Rental car fees and gas fares

D . All of the above.

Task Three Sum up the main idea of the text in 100 words.

. . . .

_____

_____

_____

_____

Part D   Reading Strategy

Identifying the Topic

The topic is the broad, general theme or message. Textbook chapters, articles, paragraphs, sentences or passages all have topics. Understanding the topic is a complex reading task. Being able to draw conclusion, evaluate and critically interpret articles or chapters is important for overall comprehension in English reading.

To know what a paragraph is mainly about, the first thing you must be able to do is identify the topic. Simply ask yourself the question, "What is this about?" Keep asking yourself that question as you read a paragraph, until the answer to your question becomes clear. Sometimes you can identify the topic by looking for a word or two that repeat. Usually you can state the topic in a few words.

Fol l ow-up Work Read the following passage and try to get the topic of the passage and that of each paragraph. The topic of the first paragraph has been given as an example. You should finish the task within 5 minutes.

1. Want to improve your English? It can be difficult for some people to do, especially non-native speakers of English. But it isn't that hard to do if you know of a few simple methods anyone can employ.

2. A very simple method of improving your English vocabulary is to buy a dictionary and read from it every day. Yes, I know this sounds pretty boring, but it's the simplest method of learning new words. Just pick up a dictionary and read a page from it every day. You will be teaching yourself new words that you can use in everyday conversation. Your vocabulary will also expand and will help you develop a subtlety to the English language you never knew existed.

3. That may be rather boring, however. For a more stimulating activity, you can read books and write down all the words you come across that you don't know the exact meaning of. Then, you

can look that word up in the dictionary and write down its definition. You can also look up those words in a thesaurus and write down its synonyms and antonyms.

4. Once basic pronunciation skills are achieved, reading poetry aloud is a good way to continue developing it. Rhyming poetry has a beat and rhythm to it that are easy to pick up intuitively. A reader only needs a few lines before they can pick up the basic rhyme scheme to the poem. Because the poem follows a standard scheme of rhyming and rhythm, it's easy for readers to pick up. Even if they don't understand the words, they can use the scheme as a guide.

5. The easiest would be to keep a simple journal or blog in which you write about the notable events of your day. Many people become intimidated writing in journals or blogs online. However, such fears can be diminished if you write only for yourself and don't publish any of your writings until you feel comfortable doing so.

6. Those are the basic ways of improving your English skills, from reading to speaking to writing. As you improve your skills, try to take on more and more challenges so you can further improve. Read longer books and magazines more. Speak more often in public by attending poetry readings. Write more articles on your interests. People never stop learning and never stop improving their skills. While it may take time to do, it is time well spent since it allows you to better communicate with and understand the people in the world around you. Improving your English skills, even little by little, will help you live a more fulfilling life in the long run.

Topic of passage: _____

Topics of the paragraphs:

Para. 1: Using methods to improve English

Para. 2: _____

Para. 3: _____

Para. 4: _____

Para. 5: _____

Para. 6: _____

Part E Banked Cloze

Direction: *In the following text, there are ten blanks. Read the text and then fill in each blank with a word from the word bank. Each choice in the bank is identified by a letter. Do not use any of the* *words more than twice.*

Travel Etiquette

Whether this will be your first or your thousandth business trip, you should be _____ (1) of conduct that is considered proper during your absence from the office. As a representative of your company, you need to know how to _____ (2) appropriately on a business trip.

First, you need to pack all the _____ (3) items in a carry-on bag to avoid being ill-prepared for business if the airline loses your luggage. Showing up for a trade show or a meeting with a client dressed in yesterday's clothes will not make a positive _____ (4). Second, you should dress professionally during the entire trip. Your attire should _____ (5) the fact that you are on a business trip, whether you are on a plane, on a golf course or in a conference room. Third, you will have to be prepared and be on time. You may normally arrive at the office at 8:10 every morning and not speak until after your first cup of coffee, but _____ (6) will not take kindly to your decision to be 10 minutes late for an important meeting and still needing to go over your notes. Fourth, you are required to use proper business language. Even _____ (7) some business trips may include more casual situations, such as lunch, dinner or even golf, keep in _____ (8) that you are still representing your company, and like the old saying goes, "Loose lips sink ships". Fifth, you should brush _____ (9) on table manners and the basics of business etiquette before you go. This may help you avoid an embarrassing gaffe while on your trip.

Last but not the least, you must save all receipts from your trip so you can easily _____ (10) your expenses when you return and conduct yourself with grace and decorum at all times.

A) essential	B) clients	C) reflect	D) behave	E) conscious
F) though	G) up	H) mind	I) determine	J) impression

Unit 7
HR Management

Part A Brainstorming

Directions: *Read the following short story and discuss the following questions.*

➢ *What can you learn from the funny story?*
➢ *What do you think of the vixen?*

The Vixen and the Lioness

A vixen who was taking her babies out for an airing one balmy morning, came across a Lioness, with her cub in arms. "Why such airs, haughty dame, over one solitary cub?" sneered the vixen. "Look at my healthy and numerous little babies here, and imagine, if you are able, how a proud mother should feel." The Lioness gave her a squelching look, and lifting up her nose, walked away, saying calmly, "Yes, just look at that beautiful collection. What are they? Foxes! I've only one, but remember, that one is a Lion."

What can you get from the story?

A. Quality is better than quantity.

B. Every coin has two sides.

C. Nothing is difficult for a strong mind.

D. Every cloud has a silver lining.

Part B Termination Procedure

Pre-reading Questions

➢ *What is the voluntary termination procedure?*

➢ *How many kinds of involuntary termination are there and what are their differences?*

1. Voluntary Termination — Resignation

Employees who intend to resign voluntarily from their position should submit a letter of resignation to their supervisor or department head specifying the reason for resignation and the last day of work. It is expected that office/support employees give a minimum of two weeks notice, and administrative/professional employees give a minimum of one month notice. More advanced notice is expected for senior level positions.

Upon receipt of the employee's resignation letter, the supervisor will record the required information on the HR/Payroll Action Form including unused accrued vacation time, and immediately send both documents to HRM for processing for timely payment of unused accrued vacation time and termination from the company. The supervisor should also provide the employee with a copy of the Employment Separation Information which contains important information for the employee as he/she is departing from the company.

2. Involuntary Termination — Reduction in Force

An administrative/professional or support staff member will be given notice of a pending reduction in force, which will result in the person's termination from the company's employment.

In order to assist a staff member in securing other employment, he/she will be given notice equal to two weeks for each full year of continuing company service (since most recent hire date) up to a maximum of six months notice. The company may grant pay in lieu of notice or a combination of notice and pay in lieu of notice as circumstances dictate.

A staff member who has been given a notice of termination due to a reduction in force will be referred to HRM for assistance in seeking other suitable company openings for which he/she may qualify.

After the decision has been made to discontinue a position, the department staff, in collaboration with HRM, will prepare a letter(s) to notify the employee(s) of the action. The supervisor will complete the HR/Payroll Action Form, to include information of unused vacation time, pay granted by the company in lieu of notice and any additional conditions.

3. Involuntary Termination — Unsatisfactory Job Performance

Administrative/professional and support staff members who fail to meet expected standards of performance and do not respond to informal counseling should be formally notified by his/her supervisor of the areas of substandard performance via the performance appraisal process and/or other written communication. If performance continues at a substandard level, additional communications, warnings, and counseling should be provided by the supervisor and HRM should be consulted by the department.

If termination of employment is considered, the department head should consult with HRM to review the circumstances and make final arrangements.

After the decision has been made to terminate an employee, the supervisor — in consultation with HRM — will prepare a letter of termination and complete the HR/Payroll Action Form for processing, including unused accrued vacation time for timely payment of unused accrued vacation time and termination from the company.

4. Involuntary Termination — Misconduct

Gross personal misconduct, gross neglect of duty or other malfeasances may result in termination without prior warning.

In such cases, the department head must consult with the appropriate Vice President and HRM to outline a specific course of action.

After the decision has been made to terminate an employee, the supervisor — in consultation with HRM — will prepare a letter of termination and complete the HR/Payroll Action Form for processing, including unused accrued vacation time, and forward to HRM for timely payment of unused accrued vacation time and termination from the company.

Task One Choose the best answer to fill in the blank.

. . . .

1. A _____ is a formal act of giving up or quitting one's office or position.

    A．resignation   B．receipt   C．designation   D．assignment

2. The dispute was brought to a satisfactory _____ .

    A．illumination   B．determination

    C．termination   D．intermediate

3. In cooking, _____ is the process of thickening and intensifying the flavor of a liquid mixture such as a soup, sauce, wine, or juice by boiling.

    A．preparation   B．reduction   C．production   D．conduction

4. I was terrified out of my mind, giving my first public _____ .

    A．maintenance   B．instance   C．performance   D．distance

5. She asked him for _____ in his office but he refused it at a word.

    A．department   B．job   C．development   D．employment

6. When in doubt about the meaning of a word, _____ a dictionary.

    A．look   B．consult   C．result   D．insult

7. The company only dismisses its employees in cases of gross _____ .

    A．misconduct   B．conduct   C．product   D．deduct

8. We have already made arrangements for our summer _____ .

    A．relation   B．vocation   C．decision   D．vacation

Task Two   Decide whether the following statements are true or false according to the text.

. . . .

1. (   ) Employees who have resigned voluntarily from their position should submit a letter of resignation to their supervisor or department head.

2. (   ) The employee should provide the supervisor with a copy of the Employment Separation Information.

3. (   ) Three kinds of involuntary termination are mentioned in the text, which are reduction in force, resignation and unsatisfactory job performance.

4. (   ) If the termination of employment is considered, the department head should not necessarily consult with HRM to review the circumstances and make final arrangements.

5. (   ) Gross personal misconduct, gross neglect of duty or other malfeasances may result in termination without prior warning.

Task Three Translate the following sentences from the text into Chinese.

1. Employees who intend to resign voluntarily from their position should submit a letter of resignation to their supervisor or department head specifying the reason for resignation and the last day of work.

2. The supervisor should also provide the employee with a copy of the Employment Separation Information which contains important information for the employee as he/she is departing from the company.

3. A staff member who has been given a notice of termination due to a reduction in force will be referred to HRM for assistance in seeking other suitable company openings for which he/she may qualify.

4. If performance continues at a substandard level, additional communications, warnings, and counseling should be provided by the supervisor and HRM should be consulted by the department.

5. In such cases, the department head must consult with the appropriate Vice President and HRM to outline a specific course of action.

Part C Internal Mobility and Transfer

Pre-reading Questions

➢ *What are the purposes of internal mobility?*
➢ *What are the purposes of transfer?*

The lateral or vertical movement (promotions, transfer demotion or separation) of an employee within an organization is called internal mobility. It may take place between jobs in various departments or divisions. Some employees may leave the organization for reasons such as better prospects, retirement terminations, etc. Such movements are known as external mobility.

Purposes of Internal Mobility:

- Improper organizational effectiveness: Organizations want to become lean and clean. To this end, structural defects may have to be eliminated; unwanted positions removed and other jobs redesigned. Internal mobility increases every such change within an organization.

- Improve the employee's effectiveness: Knowledge, skills and abilities (KSAs) can be put to use if there is a good equation between what the person has and what the organizations demand. Through promotions and transfers organizations try to bridge such gaps.

- Adjust to changing business operations: During a boom, there might be a phenomenal demand for new skills. Finance professionals were in great demand, for example during the early 90s. In a recession, layoffs may be needed to cut down and survive. Likewise short term adjustments may have to be carried out in case of death or illness of an employee.

- Ensure discipline: Demotion causes loss of status and earning capacity. A demoted employee has to learn new ways of getting things done and adjust to a new setting. Demotions can be used to ensure discipline and to correct wrong placements and job assignments.

Internal mobility as stated previously includes a cluster consisting of transfer, promotion and demotion, each of which are briefly discussed here. Separations and terminations (discharge, dismissal) which form a part of mobility in general are discussed later on.

A transfer is a change in job assignment. It may involve a promotion or demotion or change in status and responsibility. A transfer has to be viewed as a change in assignments in which an employee moves from one job to another in the same level of hierarchy requiring similar skills involving approximately same level of responsibility, same status and same level of pay. A transfer does not imply any ascending (promotion) or descending (demotion) change in status or responsibility.

Purposes of Transfer:

Organizations resort to transfers with a view to serve the following purposes:

● To meet the organizational requirements: Organizations may have to transfer employees due to changes in technology; changes in volume of productions, production schedule, product line; quality of products, changes in the job pattern caused by change in organizational structure, fluctuation in the market, conditions like demands, introduction of fewer lines and /or dropping of existing lines. All these changes demand the shift in job assignments with a view to place the right man on the right job.

● To satisfy the employees' needs: Employees may need transfers in order to satisfy their desire to work under a friendly superior, in a department / region where opportunities for advancement are bright, in or near their native place or place of interest, doing a job where the work itself is challenging.

● To utilize employees better: An employee may be transferred because management feels that his skills, experiences and job knowledge could be put to better use elsewhere.

● To make the employees more versatile: Employees may be rolled over different jobs to expand their capabilities. Job rotation may prepare the employees for more challenging assignments in future.

● To adjust the workforce: Workforce may be transferred from a plant where there is less work to a plant where there is more work.

● To provide relief: Transfer may be given to employees who are overburdened or doing hazardous work for long periods.

● To punish employees: Transfers may be effected as a disciplinary measure to shift employees indulging in undesirable activities to remote far flung areas.

Task One **Fill in the blanks with the expressions given below. Change the form when necessary.**

· ·

mobility; *effectiveness*; *promotion*; *ensure*; *transfer*; *fluctuate*; *assignment*; *utilize*; *versatile*; *relief*

1. Doubts about the _____ of secondary education also show themselves in ideas of curricular

reform.

2. How are you going to get through the _____ ?

3. The actual cost may _____ above and below that standard.

4. We're having a little get-together to celebrate David's _____ .

5. How can we _____ his knowledge and skill to our advantage?

6. Then couldn't we live in the fresh air while enjoying the _____ of cars?

7. Anton was able to _____ from Lavine's to an American company.

8. We all heaved a sigh of _____ when we heard that they were safe.

9. He's a _____ actor who has played a wide variety of parts.

10. Before traveling we must _____ the availability of petrol and oil.

Task Two Choose the best answer according to the text.

1. The text mainly talks about _____ .

   A. purposes of internal mobility

   B. the necessity of internal mobility and transfer

   C. purposes of transfer

   D. both A and C

2. The word "versatile" means _____ .

   A. capable of being classified

   B. competent in many areas and able to turn with ease from one thing to another

   C. surpassing what is common or usual or expected

   D. being out or having grown cold

3. Which of the following is NOT the purpose of internal transfer?

   A. To satisfy the employees' needs.

   B. To improve employees' effectiveness.

   C. To utilize employees better.

   D. To meet the market's requirements.

4. Which of the following is NOT included in the internal mobility?

   A. Unemployment.   B. Promotion.

   C. Demotion.   D. Transfer.

5. If management attempts to provide relief, transfer may be given to employees who _____ .

A. are satisfied about their skills, experiences and job knowledge

B. are indulging in undesirable activities

C. are overburdened or doing hazardous work for long periods

D. are loyal to the company

Task Three Sum up the main idea of the text in 100 words.

· ·

_____

_____

_____

_____

· ·

Part D Reading Strategy

Making Inferences

To guess the implied meaning in the reading material is called making inferences. The writers often tell more than they say directly in their articles. Subsequently, the readers are expected to go beyond the literal meaning to detect the unstated or unindicated meaning. It is an attempt to understand the text fully. However, inferences must be based on valid and appropriate information. Otherwise you are likely to make the wrong inferences.

Here are some strategies for making inferences:

➤ Grasp the literal meaning first. Before you make any interpretation, try to grasp the stated facts and ideas. Only when you have an understanding of the literal or factual content can you go beyond literal meaning and formulate inferences.

➤ Try to read beyond the given words. Fill in details, information and ideas based on the writer's suggestions and your own knowledge about the background of the writing.

➤ Ask questions to help you make inferences: such as, What is left out? What more is suggested?

What does the author literally say? What does the author really mean?

➤ Pay attention to the information that helps you identify the subject of the article, the author's attitudes, values and beliefs, and the author's conclusions. You often have to infer these.

➤ In inferring meaning from the context, one might say:

(1) The author implies that ...

(2) It can be easily guessed that ...

(3) The author seems to be in favor of (against) ...

(4) We can learn from the passage that ...

(5) It can be concluded from the passage that ...

(6) Which of the following can (not) be inferred from the passage?

(7) What does the article (passage) say about ...?

(8) The passage suggests that ...

(9) The author of the passage would most likely imply ...

(10) The author may probably agree with (support) ...

(11) It can be concluded that ...

(12) According to the author, what does the sentence suggest?

(13) The passage in intended to ...

(14) From the passage we can draw the conclusion that ...

(15) The tone of the passage may be ...

(16) Where would the passage most probably appear (be found)?

Follow-up Work **Read the following passages and make the inference choice.**

· ·

Passage 1

Scratchy throats, stuffy noses and body aches all spell misery, but being able to tell if the cause is a cold or flu may make a difference in how long the misery lasts.

The American Lung Association (ALA) has issued new guidelines on combating colds and the flu, and one of the keys is being able to quickly tell the two apart. That's because the prescription drugs available for the flu need to be taken soon after the illness sets in. As for colds, the sooner a person starts taking over-the-counter remedy, the sooner relief will come.

1. According to the passage, to combat the flu effectively, _____ .

   A. one should identify the virus which causes it

   B. one should consult a doctor as soon as possible

   C. one should not take medicine upon catching the disease

   D. one should remain alert when the disease is spreading

Passage 2

    Consumers are being confused and misled by the hodge-podge of environmental claims made by household products, according to a "green labeling" study published by Consumers International Friday.

    Among the report's more outrageous findings — a German fertilizer described itself as "earthworm friendly", a brand of flour said it was "non-polluting", and a British toilet paper claimed to be "environmentally friendlier".

    The study was written and researched by Britain's National Consumer Council (NCC) for lobby group Consumer International. It was funded by the German and Dutch governments and the European Commission.

    "While many good and useful claims are being made, it is clear there is a long way to go in ensuring shoppers adequately informed about the environmental impact of products they buy," said Consumers International director Anna Fielder.

1. According to the passage, the NCC found it outrageous that _____ .

   A. all the products surveyed claim to meet ISO standards

   B. the claims made by products are often unclear or deceiving

   C. consumers would believe many of the manufacturer's claims

   D. few products actually prove to be environmentally friendly

2. As indicated in this passage, with so many good claims, the consumers _____ .

   A. are becoming more cautious about the products they are going to buy

   B. are still not willing to pay more for products with green labeling

C. are becoming more aware of the effects different products have on the environment

D. still do not know the exact impact of different products on the environment

Part E Banked Cloze

Directions：

- *Read the passage about attitude of some companies to training.*
- *Choose the best sentence from the list A-G to fill in each of the blanks.*
- *Do not mark any letter twice.*

A surprisingly large number of companies still regard training as an expensive luxury. ____1____. Not surprisingly, all surveys conducted in this field have shown that the companies with the largest budgets for training are usually far more successful than those with small training budgets.

In spite of such surveys, too many business people remain suspicious of the need for training. ____2____ Even where there is an emphasis on training, the whole question of sending people on courses is often mishandled. ____3____ Although they seem happy to spend their company's money, they neglect to ask essential questions about the relevance of a particular course for their company.

Some managers specify the type of course they want for a company employee but is usually far too general. ____4____ However, this does not imply that every successful training course should meet only limited, short-term objectives： ____5____ By that time, the individual may have outgrown the need for such skills or the company itself may have changed radically. Thus it is important to have a thorough discussion with both the individual attending a course and the senior personnel in the company he or she represents. ____6____ In addition, a built-in flexibility can prove usual for equipping someone with a better understanding of new skills and fresh approaches as technologies change or as the employee's job changes.

A. Such business people argue that they have managed their companies very successfully without any training at all.

B． Unfortunately，a number of managers，for instance，rush into this whole matter without enough careful thought beforehand.

C． In this way，both short-term and long-term skills may be identified.

D． On the other hand，they refuse to pay considerable sums to send their staff on courses.

E． Where this is the case，the management skills acquired may be inappropriate after a few years.

F． Too often they want a course aimed at an ill-defined average group rather than at specific development needs.

G． In spite of such objectives，a training course can be very successful in meeting future needs.

1. ☐A ☐B ☐C ☐D ☐E ☐F ☐G
2. ☐A ☐B ☐C ☐D ☐E ☐F ☐G
3. ☐A ☐B ☐C ☐D ☐E ☐F ☐G
4. ☐A ☐B ☐C ☐D ☐E ☐F ☐G
5. ☐A ☐B ☐C ☐D ☐E ☐F ☐G
6. ☐A ☐B ☐C ☐D ☐E ☐F ☐G

Unit 8
Cash Management

Matrix

- Budget
- Cash flow

Part A Brainstorming

Directions: *Read the following short story and discuss the following questions.*

➢ *What can you learn from the funny story?*

➢ *What do you think of the widow?*

The Widow and the Sheep

A certain poor widow had one solitary sheep. At shearing time, wishing to take his fleece and to avoid expense, she sheared him herself, but used the shears so unskillfully that with the fleece she sheared the flesh. The sheep, writhing with pain, said, "Why do you hurt me so, Mistress? What weight can my blood add to the wool? If you want my flesh, there is the butcher, who will kill me in an instant; but if you want my fleece and wool, there is the shearer, who will shear and not hurt me."

1. What can you get from the story?

A. Practice makes perfect.

B. The least outlay is not always the greatest gain.

C. No pains, no gains.

D. Perseverance prevails.

Part B What Are the Steps in the Budget Process?

Pre-reading Questions

➤ *How many basic steps are there in the budget process?*

The first step in the budget process is a review of program and management achievements and fiscal performance over the year just ending. This includes, but is not limited to, reviewing objectives achieved, comparing budget to actual figures, and looking at the number of people served in each program. By dividing the true cost of each program and by the number of people served, you can also analyze the cost per unit of service. Based on this review, new goals and objectives should be discussed and agreed upon in a preliminary way. These goals and objectives should fit into your strategic, long-range plan, and help you make progress towards your mission.

Then, estimate the costs required to achieve your objectives, including staff, supplies, and other resources. Include both program and financial staff in discussions of programmatic costs to make sure that all resources required by programs are considered. Management staff should be included in discussions for their own departmental budgets and how these relate to programmatic objectives.

You must budget for income as well as expenses. Even though unpredictable events may influence fees and contributions, you can estimate revenues with some degree of accuracy based on past experience. As with any budgeting based on the past, it is important to make adjustments for future plans and changes when you have sufficient information to anticipate. The financial and fundraising staff, in collaboration with the executive director and fundraising committee of the board, have to make the most realistic assessment possible for budgeting purposes. It may also be useful to develop contingency budgets for more conservative or optimistic projections of revenue.

Finally, compare revenue and expense projections. At different times organizations will choose to incur a deficit, realize a surplus, or simply break even. No rule says that budgets must balance in each budget period. Certainly, large deficits can lead to bankruptcy, and large surpluses may mean that the organization is not investing enough of its revenues in serving the public interest. However, for any given budget period, revenue and expenses should be in the relationship that the organization chooses, rather than mechanically "balanced".

If a preliminary budget has been prepared and revenue and expenses are not in the desired relationship, programs and management activities must be reevaluated and adjustments made. When reviewing the revenue budget, it is important to avoid the temptation of raising the estimate without changing the plans for generating revenue. The budget should be based on reasonable assumptions you have some grounds for making. Typically, nonprofit organizations find that their initial projections for income and expenses anticipate an unacceptable deficit, and either additional revenue must be generated or activities must be cut back.

Task One   Choose the best answer to fill in the blank.

· ·

1. She will design a fantastic new kitchen for you — and all within your _____ .

   A. facility   B. budget   C. expense   D. project

2. May I make a few _____ remarks before we start the interview?

   A. prime   B. primary   C. preliminary   D. fundamental

3. I don't know her well enough to form an _____ of her abilities.

   A. eliminate   B. predicate   C. estimate   D. mediate

4. Undoubtedly the generals feared the _____ consequences.

   A. understandable   B. impossible

   C. unpredictable   D. unrecoverable

5. My own _____ is that the person in yellow is superior to the man in blue.

   A. recess   B. assessment   C. process   D. confession

6. The manufacturers in some countries dumped their _____ commodities abroad.

   A. deficient   B. salable   C. qualified   D. surplus

7. The government's _____ is made up chiefly of the money we pay in taxes.

   A. wage   B. salary   C. income   D. revenue

8. Tax was low and state spending was high, resulting in a budget _____ .

   A. expense   B. loss   C. deficit   D. cost

Task Two　Decide whether the following statements are true or false according to the text.

. . . .

1. (　　) The most important step in the budget process is a review of program and management achievements and fiscal performance over the year just ending.

2. (　　) Only for some given budget periods, revenue and expenses should be in the relationship that the organization chooses, rather than mechanically "balanced".

3. (　　) It is possibly useful to develop contingency budgets for more conservative or optimistic projections of revenue.

4. (　　) Management staff should not be excluded in discussions for their own departmental budgets and how these relate to programmatic objectives.

5. (　　) The budget should be founded on reasonable assumptions you have some grounds for making.

Task Three　Translate the following sentences from the text into Chinese.

. . . .

1. By dividing the true cost of each program by the number of people served, you can also analyze the cost per unit of service.

_____

_____

2. Even though unpredictable events may influence fees and contributions, you can estimate revenues with some degree of accuracy based on past experience.

_____

_____

3. It may also be useful to develop contingency budgets for more conservative or optimistic projections of revenue.

_____

_____

4. Certainly, large deficits can lead to bankruptcy, and large surpluses may mean that the organization is not investing enough of its revenues in serving the public interest.

5. If a preliminary budget has been prepared and revenue and expenses are not in the desired relationship, programs and management activities must be reevaluated and adjustments made.

Part C   The Essentials of Corporate Cash Flow

Pre-reading Questions

➢ *What are the essentials of corporate cash flow?*

➢ *What cannot we learn from cash flow?*

If a company reports earnings of $1 billion, does this mean it has this amount of cash in the bank? Not necessarily. Financial statements are based on accrual accounting, which takes into account non-cash items. It does this in an effort to best reflect the financial health of a company. However, accrual accounting may create accounting noise, which sometimes needs to be tuned out so that it's clear how much actual cash a company is generating. The statement of cash flow provides this information, and here we look at what cash flow is and how to read the cash flow statement.

What Is Cash Flow?

Business is all about trade, the exchange of value between two or more parties, and cash is the asset needed for participation in the economic system. For this reason — while some industries are more cash intensive than others — no business can survive in the long run without generating positive cash flow per share for its shareholders. To have a positive cash flow, the company's long-term cash inflows need to exceed its long-term cash outflows.

An outflow of cash occurs when a company transfers funds to another party (either physically or electronically). Such a transfer could be made to pay for employees, suppliers and creditors, or to purchase long-term assets and investments, or even pay for legal expenses and lawsuit settlements. It is important to note that legal transfers of value through debt — a purchase made on credit — is not recorded as a cash outflow until the money actually leaves the company's hands.

A cash inflow is of course the exact opposite; it is any transfer of money that comes into the company's possession. Typically, the majority of a company's cash inflows are from customers, lenders (such as banks or bondholders) and investors who purchase company equity from the company. Occasionally cash flows come from sources like legal settlements or the sale of company's real estate or equipment.

What is the Cash Flow Statement?

There are three important parts of a company's financial statements: the balance sheet, the income statement and the cash flow statement. The balance sheet gives a one-time snapshot of a company's assets and liabilities. And the income statement indicates the business's profitability during a certain period.

The cash flow statement differs from these other financial statements because it acts as a kind of corporate checkbook that reconciles the other two statements. Simply put, the cash flow statement records the company's cash transactions (the inflows and outflows) during the given period. It shows whether all those lovely revenues booked on the income statement have actually been collected. At the same time, however, remember that the cash flow does not necessarily show all the company's expenses: not all expenses the company accrues have to be paid right away. So even though the company may have incurred liabilities it must eventually pay, expenses are not recorded as a cash outflow until they are paid.

When you look at a cash flow statement, the first thing you should look at is the bottom line item that says something like "net increase/decrease in cash and cash equivalents", since this line reports the overall change in the company's cash and its equivalents (the assets that can be immediately converted into cash) over the last period. If you check under current assets on the balance sheet, you will find cash and cash equivalents (CCE or CC&E). If you take the difference between the current CCE and last year's or last quarter's, you'll get this same number found at the bottom of the statement of cash flows.

What Cash Flow Doesn't Tell Us

Cash is one of the major lubricants of business activity, but there are certain things that cash flow doesn't shed light on. For example, as we explained above, it doesn't tell us the profit earned or lost during a particular period: profitability is composed also of things that are not cash based. This is true even for numbers on the cash flow statement like "cash increase from sales minus expenses", which may sound like they are indication of profit but are not.

As it doesn't tell the whole profitability story, cash flow doesn't do a very good job of indicating the overall financial well-being of the company. Sure, the statement of cash flow indicates what the company is doing with its cash and where cash is being generated, but these do not reflect the company's entire financial condition. The cash flow statement does not account for liabilities and assets, which are recorded on the balance sheet. Furthermore accounts receivable and accounts payable, each of which can be very large for a company, are also not reflected in the cash flow statement.

In other words, the cash flow statement is a compressed version of the company's checkbook that includes a few other items that affect cash, like the financing section, which shows how much the company spent or collected from the repurchase or sale of stock, the amount of issuance or retirement of debt and the amount the company paid out in dividends.

Task One Fill in the blanks with the expressions given below. Change the form when necessary.

· ·

financial; accounting; in the long run; exceed; assets; accrue; equivalents; lubricant; shed light on; compress

1. If your liabilities _____ your assets, you may go bankrupt.
2. English skills will _____ to you from speaking and reading a lot.
3. If the company continues on this course, it's heading for _____ trouble.
4. A company's _____ records must be open for inspection at all times.
5. Many people use personal _____ as collateral for small business loans.
6. Humor is a great _____ for teamwork.
7. She has told them nothing that could _____ her husband's whereabouts.
8. Avoiding danger is no safer _____ than outright exposure.

9. It's impossible to _____ this mass of material into a few pages.

10. Cash and cash _____ are carried in the balance sheet at cost.

Task Two Choose the best answer according to the text.

. . . .

1. The text mainly talks about _____ .

   A. the company's long-term cash inflows exceeding its long term cash outflows

   B. the definition of cash flow and the way to read cash flow statement

   C. three important parts of a company's financial statements

   D. those things cash flow does not shed light on

2. The word "lubricant" means _____ .

   A. management by overseeing the performance or operation of a person or group

   B. produced or growing in extreme abundance

   C. the property of being smooth and shiny

   D. a substance capable of reducing friction by making surfaces smooth or slippery

3. Which of the following is NOT included in a company's financial statements?

   A. The balance sheet.

   B. The income statement.

   C. The professional statement.

   D. The cash flow statement.

4. The cash flow statement differs from the other financial statements in that _____ .

   A. it gives a one-time snapshot of a company's assets and liabilities

   B. it indicates the business's profitability during a certain period

   C. it acts as a kind of corporate checkbook that reconciles the other two statements

   D. it comes from sources like legal settlements or the sale of company's real estate

5. According to the text, we can infer that _____ .

   A. the cash flow statement is a compressed version of the company's checkbook

   B. the bottomline of a cash flow statement reports the overall change in the company's cash and its equivalents over the last period

   C. we cannot find the overall financial well-being of the company by reading the statement of cash flow

   D. cash flow tells us the profit earned or lost during a particular period

Task Three **Sum up the main idea of the text in 100 words.**

....

_____

_____

_____

_____

....

Part D   Reading Strategy

Understanding Text Structures

When reading, one usually encounters two kinds of texts — narrative and expository. Narrative text typically follows a single general structural pattern often called "story grammar". In this kind of text, one should try to locate the time, place, circumstances, and main characters.

Expository or information text conveys and communicates factual information. This type of text generally contains more unfamiliar vocabulary and concepts. It also has fewer ideas related to personal experience, as well as a variety of structures. There are several patterns of expository text: description/list, cause/effect, comparison/contrast, order/ sequence, and problem/solution.

How should one understand text structures? The following chart can help identify the structures of expository texts.

Text Structure	Description	Signal Words
Description & List	This structure resembles an outline. Each section opens with its main idea, elaborates on it, and then sometimes divides the elaboration into subsections.	for example for instance specifically in particular in addition

续 表

Text Structure	Description	Signal Words
Cause & Effect	Texts that follow this structure tell the reader the result of an event or occurrence and the reasons why it happened.	consequently therefore as a result thereby lead to
Comparison & Contrast	Texts that follow this structure explain differences and similarities among two or more objects, places, events, or ideas by grouping their traits for comparison.	however unlike like in contrast yet in comparison although whereas similar to different from
Order & Sequence	Texts that follow this structure show the order in which steps in a process or series of events occur.	next first last second another then additionally
Problem & Solution	The author presents a problem, followed by one or more solutions.	problem is dilemma is if/then because so that question answer puzzle is solved

Follow-up Work Complete the following passages by choosing the proper signal words given in the box. Capitalize the initial letter when necessary.

Exercise 1

first; or; second; when; however; therefore; consequently; because; then; although

One can write short, one-act plays or long plays with two or more acts. Each act may have more than one scene, especially if there needs to be a change of costumes, props, or sets. (1)_____ writing a play, use many of the ideas already mentioned — plot, character, and dialogue. (2)_____ there are two main differences between a play and a story. (3)_____, in a play one depends completely on dialogue to convey the plot and the characters. (4)_____, (5)_____ a play is meant to be acted out on a stage, one has to write stage directions: what the characters should do while they are on stage, as well as what they should say.

Exercise 2

> *firstly*; *or*; *secondly*; *when*; *like*; *therefore*; *however*; *because*; *then*; *thirdly*

When we reduce overheads, less advertising, hiring part-time or unpaid workers and saving energy should be considered. ____1____, companies usually spend too much in advertising. It may be the first to be cut because it can be reduced almost instantly. And companies can also resort to the power of the internet. It will make advertising less wasteful. ____2____, hiring part-time or unpaid workers will save a lot of staff cost for the company. Companies can hire some people ____3____ college students to be the part-time workers, less paid or unpaid. ____4____, saving energy is also important because it will save a large sum of money. So, companies should set up some rules to save the power, water, paper and the like. ____5____, all the three aspects are important when reducing overheads.

Part E Banked Cloze

Directions:

- *Read the passage about website term paper.*
- *Choose the best sentence from the list A-I to fill in each of the blanks.*
- *Do not mark any letter twice.*

For generations of students, writing term papers has been a major source of nerves and frustration, if not the ultimate homework nightmare: ____1____.

      2   All one has to do is to go to the appropriate website, where online papers can either be purchased, ordered, or downloaded for free.

If you are too lazy or simply too busy writing your own term paper, Genius Papers is readily available. _____3_____. Some sites, such as Term Paper Emporium and Absolutely Free: Online Essays offer course papers for free. Simply click the mouse and download — if you find the paper you want, that is.

Students are, of course, fully aware of these website resources. _____4_____

For teachers, the problem is figuring out whether a student's authorship is authentic. But, as teaching assistant Jane Morrison explained, _____5_____.

Faking term papers is nothing new, and stolen intellectual property has been marketed for years. But the appearance of the Internet raises the issue: _____6_____

"If you structure the assignment in a creative way, and if students, for instance, have to transform the information into a hand-out, or do a drama, or write an account in first person narrative, then you may curb illicit work," said library media teacher Leslie Farmer.

A. That kind of strategy will basically force students to do more than simply download their education.

B. Do you want to "write" a paper on "Hamlet's irreconcilable moral dilemmas"?

C. The contemporary student who wants to fake a term paper does not have to search far.

D. the task may be too difficult for the teacher to figure all out.

E. Inventive teachers can make their assignments almost cheat-proof.

F. But for those with Internet access, illicit resources are just a few links away.

G. Is this new technology making cheating more widespread?

H. And some people worry that the Internet could become the best aid yet for cheating.

I. For a one-time fee of $9.95, you get access to pre-written papers for an entire semester.

---

1. ☐A ☐B ☐C ☐D ☐E ☐F ☐G ☐H ☐I
2. ☐A ☐B ☐C ☐D ☐E ☐F ☐G ☐H ☐I
3. ☐A ☐B ☐C ☐D ☐E ☐F ☐G ☐H ☐I
4. ☐A ☐B ☐C ☐D ☐E ☐F ☐G ☐H ☐I
5. ☐A ☐B ☐C ☐D ☐E ☐F ☐G ☐H ☐I
6. ☐A ☐B ☐C ☐D ☐E ☐F ☐G ☐H ☐I

Unit 9

Financial Management

Matrix

- Breakeven point
- Balance of payments

Part A Brainstorming

Directions: *Read the following short story and fill in the blank. And then discuss the following questions.*

➢ *What can you learn from the funny story?*

➢ *What do you think of the interviewer?*

Account

Fresh out of business school, the young man answered a want ad for an accountant. Now he was being interviewed by a very nervous man who ran a small business that he had started himself.

"I need someone with an accounting degree," the man said, "but mainly, I'm looking for someone to do my worrying for me."

"Excuse me?" the accountant said.

"I worry about a lot of things," the man said, "but I don't want to have to worry about money. Your job will be to take all the money worries off my back."

"I see," the accountant said, "and how much does the job pay?"

"I'll start you at eighty thousand."

"Eighty thousand dollars!" the accountant exclaimed, "how can such a small business afford a sum like that?"

"That," the owner said, "_____."

The following information may do help to expand your thinking perspective:

1. Why does the interviewer ask for someone to take all the money worries off his back?

2. In your opinion, would the young man accept the job? Why or why not?

Part B Determining Your Breakeven Point

Pre-reading Questions

➢ *What is the breakeven point?*

➢ *How do you determine your breakeven point?*

How many units — products or hours of service — do you have to sell to cover your costs? Don't know? Then it's about time you found out! Follow these five steps for figuring out your breakeven point. It's the key to determining your pricing and profitability.

1. Determine the pre-unit selling price and direct costs

Direct costs are classified as the costs that go into creating the product or service (that is, direct materials and direct labor). So let's say you have a gift basket business. The direct costs would be the price of the basket, the items in the basket, the wrap for the basket, and the labor involved in putting the basket together.

2. Calculate your contribution margin in dollars per unit

Once you know the selling price and direct costs of each product or service unit you sell, you can calculate your contribution margin in dollars per unit. This is the amount of money you get over and above your direct costs for each unit you sell. (You can define your unit as either a product or hour of service.) Again, using the gift basket business as an example, if your selling price was $50 and your direct costs added up to $40, then your contribution margin in dollars would be $10 per unit. This is the amount you can contribute towards your overhead costs from each sale of your product or service.

3. Calculate your overhead costs

What are all the other costs you incur in your business that need to be covered before you can start earning a profit? Overhead costs include such things as insurance, indirect labor rent, taxes, dues and subscriptions, advertising, office supplies and so on. This is calculated in total, not on a per-unit basis. You need to know how much money it takes to run your business because you've got to cover these costs in addition to your direct costs before you can start making a profit.

4. Determine your breakeven point

Once you know your overhead costs, take that total number and divide it by your contribution margin in dollars per unit (the answer from Step 2 above). For example, if your overhead costs were $1,000 and your contribution margin from each unit you sell is $10, then your breakeven in units would be $1,000/$10 or 100 units. So, continuing with the gift basket business example, you must sell 100 gift baskets at $50 each to break even. Remember, there's no profit in your business until you've covered your direct and indirect (overhead) expenses. Only after selling 100 units will you break even. Starting with the 101st unit, you'll be earning a profit. If you've determined that, based upon market predictions, you can only sell 40 items per month, you'll never earn a profit and you need to reconsider your business idea or your pricing. Increasing your pricing and trying to trim costs may just increase your contribution and profitability margins enough to keep you in business.

5. Recalculate your breakeven point on a regular basis

As your selling price, direct costs and indirect costs change, so will your breakeven point. So it's absolutely imperative that you recalculate it as the other costs of doing business change. Without knowing your breakeven point, you'll never know just what you have to do to make a profit.

Calculating your breakeven point is something you need to incorporate as part of your pricing policy to ensure that you're making money on every unit you sell and that you'll be able to be profitable based on your costs and your sales. If you're not profitable, you will not stay in business. It's as simple as that.

Every type of business can incorporate this equation into their pricing module. No matter whether you own a service — or product-based business, you've got to have a good understanding of your direct and indirect costs and how they affect your pricing and profitability models. It might just mean the difference between a profitable and non-profitable year for you.

If you don't know your breakeven point, you're running your business blindly. It's a fact that thousands of companies go out of business every year. Why? One decisive factor is they just don't know their numbers. Why not make a difference in your business this year and get to know your breakeven point?

Task One Choose the best answer to fill in the blank.

. . . .

1. The global economic climate and our current business conditions require AMD to readjust our _____ point and topline targets.

   A. breakdown

   B. breakeven

   C. breakthrough

   D. breakup

2. Although superstitions _____ beliefs and practices, they are usually transmitted as sayings.

   A. revolve   B. evolve   C. involve   D. devolve

3. He received honors and awards from the government for his _____ to agricultural production.

   A. distribution   B. attribution   C. contribution   D. tribute

4. Once the cargo has been shipped, _____ can be covered instantaneously.

   A. sure   B. assurance   C. insurance   D. certainty

5. Labor cost also includes general and administrative _____ and employee benefits.

   A. ahead   B. overhead   C. headache   D. heading

6. Low levels of _____ mean there is a lack of incentive to undertake new investment.

   A. cash   B. capital   C. salary   D. profitability

7. Come as intellectual economy, company finance affairs show more and more apparent inelasticity. Financial innovation is _____.

   A. complex   B. redundant   C. competitive   D. imperative

8. We shall try to _____ some of your ideas in our future plan.

   A. cooperate   B. corporate   C. incorporate   D. operate

Task Two   Decide whether the following statements are true or false according to the text.

· ·

1. (   ) Direct costs are classified as the costs that go into consuming the product or service.
2. (   ) If your selling price was $40 and your direct costs added up to $50, then your contribution margin in dollars would be $10 per unit.
3. (   ) Overhead costs include such things as insurance, indirect labor rent, taxes, dues and subscriptions, advertising, office supplies and so on.
4. (   ) Your contribution and profitability margins may be increased enough to keep you in business by increasing your pricing and trying to trim costs.
5. (   ) One decisive reason why thousands of companies go out of business every year is that they don't know their breakeven points.

Task Three   Translate the following sentences from the text into Chinese.

· ·

1. The direct costs would be the price of the basket, the items in the basket, the wrap for the basket, and the labor involved in putting the basket together.

_____

_____

2. Once you know the selling price and direct costs of each product or service unit you sell, you can calculate your contribution margin in dollars per unit.

_____

_____

3. You need to know how much money it takes to run your business because you've got to cover these costs in addition to your direct costs before you can start making a profit.

_____

_____

4. Increasing your pricing and trying to trim costs may just increase your contribution and profitability margins enough to keep you in business.

_____

5. Calculating your breakeven point is something you need to incorporate as part of your pricing policy to ensure that you're making money on every unit you sell and that you'll be able to be profitable based on your costs and your sales.

Part C Balance of Payments

Pre-reading Questions

➤ *What is the balance of payments?*

➤ *How many categories is the balance of payments mainly divided into?*

The balance of payments (BOP) is the method countries use to monitor all international monetary transactions at a specific period of time. Usually, the BOP is calculated every quarter and every calendar year. All trades conducted by both the private and public sectors are accounted for in the BOP in order to determine how much money is going in and out of a country. If a country has received money, this is known as a credit, and, if a country has paid or given money, the transaction is counted as a debit. Theoretically, the BOP should be zero, meaning that assets (credits) and liabilities (debits) should balance. But in practice this is rarely the case and, thus, the BOP can tell the observer if a country has a deficit or a surplus and from which part of the economy the discrepancies are stemming.

The Balance of Payments Divided

The BOP is divided into three main categories: the current account, the capital account and the financial account. Within these three categories are sub-divisions, each of which accounts for a different type of international monetary transaction.

The Current Account

The current account is used to mark the inflow and outflow of goods and services into a country. Earnings on investments, both public and private, are also put into the current account.

Within the current account are credits and debits on the trade of merchandise, which includes goods such as raw materials and manufactured goods that are bought, sold or given away (possibly in the form of aid). Services refer to receipts from tourism, transportation (like the levy that must be paid in Egypt when a ship passes through the Suez Canal), engineering, business service fees (from lawyers or management consulting, for example), and royalties from patents and copyrights. When combined, goods and services together make up a country's balance of trade (BOT). The BOT is typically the biggest bulk of a country's balance of payments as it makes up total imports and exports. If a country has a balance of trade deficit, it imports more than it exports, and if it has a balance of trade surplus, it exports more than it imports.

Receipts from income-generating assets such as stocks (in the form of dividends) are also recorded in the current account. The last component of the current account is unilateral transfers. These are credits that are mostly worker's remittances, which are salaries sent back into the home country of a national working abroad, as well as foreign aid that is directly received.

The Capital Account

The capital account is where all international capital transfers are recorded. This refers to the acquisition or disposal of non-financial assets (for example, a physical asset such as land) and non-produced assets, which are needed for production but have not been produced, like a mine used for the extraction of diamonds.

The capital account is broken down into the monetary flows branching from debt forgiveness, the transfer of goods, and financial assets by migrants leaving or entering a country, the transfer of ownership on fixed assets (assets such as equipment used in the production process to generate income), the transfer of funds received to the sale or acquisition of fixed assets, gifts and inheritance taxes, death levies, and, finally, uninsured damage to fixed assets.

The Financial Account

In the financial account, international monetary flows related to investment in business, real estate, bonds and stocks are documented. Also included are government-owned assets such as foreign reserves, gold, special drawing rights (SDRs) held with the International Monetary Fund, private assets held abroad, and direct foreign investment. Assets owned by foreigners, private and official, are also recorded in the financial account.

The Balancing Act

The current account should be balanced against the combined-capital and financial accounts. However, as mentioned above, this rarely happens. We should also note that, with fluctuating exchange rates, the change in the value of money can add to BOP discrepancies. When there is a deficit in the current account, which is a balance of trade deficit, the difference can be borrowed or funded by the capital account. If a country has a fixed asset abroad, this borrowed amount is marked as a capital account outflow. However, the sale of that fixed asset would be considered a current account inflow (earnings from investments). The current account deficit would thus be funded.

When a country has a current account deficit that is financed by the capital account, the country is actually foregoing capital assets for more goods and services. If a country is borrowing money to fund its current account deficit, this would appear as an inflow of foreign capital in the BOP.

Task One　Fill in the blanks with the expressions given below. Change the form when necessary.

. . . .

transaction; debit; discrepancy; remittance; disposal; extraction; inheritance; exchange; current; capital

1. Further theoretical refinements have removed the _____ .
2. In view of our longstanding business relationship, we can conclude the _____ .
3. He placed unreservedly all the data he has collected at my _____ .
4. We undercharge Mr. Smith and have to send him a _____ note for the extra amount.
5. I don't understand television's _____ obsession with cookery programmes.
6. We hold the merchandise in readiness to ship upon receipt of your _____ .
7. Research is also advanced by frequent conference to _____ experience.

8. It's unwise to tie up all your _____ in one enterprise.

9. Chinese literature is a rich _____ of the Chinese people.

10. The local economy is overwhelmingly dependent on oil and gas _____ .

Task Two Choose the best answer according to the text.

1. According to the text, the balance of payments is _____ .

   A. the method countries use to monitor all international monetary transactions all the time

   B. the measure countries use to monitor all international monetary transactions at a specific period of time

   C. the way countries control certain international monetary transactions

   D. the approach countries develop their depressed economy

2. Which of the following is NOT one of the main categories of the BOP?

   A. The current account.   B. The capital account.

   C. The financial account.   D. The budgeting account.

3. _____ is the biggest bulk of a country's balance of payments.

   A. Investment   B. Trade surplus

   C. The balance of trade   D. Trade deficit

4. _____ refers to the acquisition or disposal of non-financial assets and non-produced assets.

   A. The current account   B. The financial account

   C. The capital account   D. The balancing act

5. The passage is mainly about _____ .

   A. efficiency of the balance of payments

   B. necessity of the balance of payments

   C. categories of the balance of payments

   D. functions of the balance of payments

Task Three Sum up the main idea of the text in 100 words.

Part D   Reading Strategy

Categorizing Information

When reading, one naturally puts information into certain categories without realizing it. This process is called categorizing information. Categorizing involves grouping objects or ideas according to criteria that describe common features or relationships among all items. This procedure enables one to see patterns and connections; it enhances one's ability to manage or organize information.

Categorizing information is important because it can:

➢ provide an opportunity to share existing knowledge and understanding

➢ extend thinking and understanding by requiring one to organize ideas and incorporate new ones

➢ encourage one to accept and understand diverse ideas and viewpoints

➢ demonstrate that information can be grouped or classified in more than one way

How could one best categorize information?

When reading a passage, ask the following questions:

➢ How are these ideas similar? How are these ideas different?

➢ Which ideas belong together? How are these ideas related to each other?

➢ How can the facts be grouped?

➢ Does the author try to show how things are similar, different, or both similar and different?

➢ What are the differing opinions on this issue shown in this passage?

This reading strategy helps one read critically and form his own categories based on the information from the passage.

Fol l ow-up Work **Read the passage and choose the best answer to each question.**

Soccer is played by millions of people all over the world, but there have only been a few players who were truly great. How did these players get that way — was it through training and practice, or are great players "born, not made"? First, these players came from places that have had famous stars in the past — players that a young boy can look up to and try to imitate. In the history of soccer, only seven countries have ever won the World Cup — three from South America and four from Western Europe. There has never been a great national team — or a really great player — from North America or from Asia. Second, these players have all had years of practice in the game. Alfredo Di Stefano was the son of a soccer player, as was Pele. Most players begin playing the game at the age of three or four.

Finally, many great players come from the same kind of neighborhood — a poor, crowded area where a boy's dream is not to be a doctor, lawyer, or businessman, but to become a rich, famous athlete or entertainer. For example, Liverpool, which produced the Beatles, had one of the best English soccer teams in recent years. Pele practiced in the street with a "ball" made of rags. And George Best learned the tricks that made him famous by bouncing the ball off a wall in the slums of Belfast.

All great players have a lot in common, but that doesn't explain why they are great. Hundreds of boys played in those Brazilian streets, but only one became Pele. The greatest players are born with unique quality that sets them apart from all the others.

1. The word "tricks" at the end of Para. 2 is closest in meaning to _____ .

   A. experience   B. cheating

   C. skills   D. raining

2. To get the way for a great player, a series of factors are directly mentioned, except _____ .

   A. age and birth

   B. family and neighborhood

   C. training and practice

   D. personality and character

Part E Banked Cloze

Directions:

- *Read the passage about Dave's dream.*
- *Choose the best sentence from the list A-G to fill in each of the blanks.*
- *Do not mark any letter twice.*

Icon Acoustics: Bypassing Tradition

Like most entrepreneurs, Dave Fokos dreams a lot. He imagines customers eagerly phoning Icon Acoustics in Billerica, Massachusetts, to order his latest, custom-made stereo speakers. ____1____.

Like most entrepreneurs, Dave has taken a long time to develop his dream. ____2____ Dave discovered that he had a strong interest in audio engineering. He took independent-study courses in this area and by graduation had designed and built a pair of marketable stereo speakers. Following graduation, Dave pursued interest in audio engineering. He landed a job as a loudspeaker designer with Conrad-Johnson, a high-end audio-equipment manufacturer headquartered in Fairfax, Virginia ____3____.

Dave identified a market niche that he felt other speaker firms had overlooked. ____4____ These affluent, well-educated customers are genuinely obsessed with their stereo equipment. "They'd rather buy a new set of speakers than eat," Dave observed.

Dave faced on major problem — how to distribute Icon's products. He had learned from experience at Conrad-Johnson that most manufacturers distribute their equipment primarily through stereo dealers. Dave did not hold a high opinion of most such dealers; he felt that they too often played hardball with manufacturers, forcing them to accept thin margins. ____5____ This kept those firms that offered more customized products from gaining access to the market. Dave felt that the established dealers often sold not what was best for customers, but whatever they had in inventory that month.

Dave dreamed of offering high-end stereo loudspeakers directly to the audio-obsessed bypassing the established dealer network. ____6____ "My vision for the future is one where all manufacturers sell their products directly to end users. In this way, even the audiophiles in Dead Horse, Alaska, can have access to all that the audio-manufacturing community has to offer."

A. At the age of 28, Dave set out to turn his dreams into reality.

B. Furthermore, the dealers concentrated on only a handful of well-know producers.

C. Who provided mass-produced models.

D. The firms tended to pour their money in to developing their products and had little leftover to market them.

E. This niche consists of "audio-addicts" — people who love to listen to music and appreciate first-rate stereo equipment.

F. To serve the audio-addicts segment, Dave offers only the highest-quality speakers.

G. It all began while majoring in electrical engineering at Cornell. By going directly to the customers, Dave could avoid the dealer markups and offer top-quality products and service at a reasonable price.

1. ☐A ☐B ☐C ☐D ☐E ☐F ☐G
2. ☐A ☐B ☐C ☐D ☐E ☐F ☐G
3. ☐A ☐B ☐C ☐D ☐E ☐F ☐G
4. ☐A ☐B ☐C ☐D ☐E ☐F ☐G
5. ☐A ☐B ☐C ☐D ☐E ☐F ☐G
6. ☐A ☐B ☐C ☐D ☐E ☐F ☐G

Unit 10
Marketing Management

Part A Brainstorming

Directions: *Read the following short story and fill in the blank. And then discuss the following questions.*

· ·

➢ *What do we learn from the story?*
➢ *What role does the Email in this story imply in real life?*

A jobless man applied for the position of "office boy" at Microsoft. The HR manager interviewed him then watched him cleaning the floor as a test.

"You are employed," he said. "Give me your email address and I'll send you the application to fill in, as well as the date when you may start."

The man replied, "But I don't have a computer, neither an email."

"I'm sorry," said the HR manager. "If you don't have an email, that means you do not exist. And who doesn't exist, cannot have the job."

The man left with no hope at all. He didn't know what to do, with only 10 dollars in his pocket. He then decided to go to the supermarket and buy a 10kg-tomato crate. He then sold the tomatoes in a door to door round. In less than two hours, he succeeded in doubling his capital. He repeated the operation three times, and returned home with 60 dollars.

The man realized that he can survive by this way, and started to go every day earlier, and return late. Thus, his money doubled or tripled every day. Shortly, he bought a cart, then a truck, and then he had his own fleet of delivery vehicles. Five years later, the man is one of the biggest food retailers in the U.S..

He started to plan his family's future, and decided to have a life insurance. He called an insurance broker, and chose a protection plan. When the conversation was concluded the broker asked him his email. The man replied, "I don't have an email."

The broker answered curiously, "You don't have an email, and yet have succeeded in building an empire. Can you imagine what you could have been if you had an email?" The man thought for a while and replied, "_____"

The following information may do help to expand your thinking perspective:

1. Imagine the end of the story if the man had done what the HR manager told him?
2. Why does the man insist on not applying for an email address?

Part B Connecting Customers

Pre-reading Questions

➢ *Are today's customers harder to please than before?*
➢ *What is more important, satisfied customers or loyal customers?*

Attracting customers

Companies seeking to grow their profits and sales have to spend considerable time and resources searching for new customers. Customer acquisition requires substantial skills in lead generation, lead qualification, and account conversion. To generate leads, the company develops ads and places them in media that will reach new prospects; it sends direct mail and makes phone calls to possible new prospects; its salespeople participate in trade shows where they might find new leads; and so on. All this activity produces a list of suspects. The next task is to qualify which of the suspects are really good prospects, and this is done by interviewing them, checking on their financial standing, and so on. The prospects may be graded as hot, warm, and cool. The sales-people first contact the hot prospects and work on account conversion, which involves making presentations, answering objections, and negotiating final terms.

Customer value

Our premise is that customers will buy from the firm that they perceive offers the highest customer delivered value. Customer delivered value is the difference between total customer value and total customer cost. Total customer value is the bundle of benefits customers expect from a given product or service. Total customer cost is the bundle of costs customers expect to incur in evaluating, obtaining, using, and disposing of the product or service.

Many companies are intent on developing stronger bonds and loyalty with their ultimate customers. In the past, many companies took their customers for granted. Their customers may not have had many alternative sources of supply, or all suppliers were equally deficient in service, or the market was growing so fast that the company did not worry about satisfying its customers. Clearly, things have changed. Today's customers are harder to please. They are smarter, more price conscious, more demanding, less forgiving, and approached by more competitors with equal or better offers. The challenge, according to Jeffrey Gitomer, is not to produce satisfied customers; several competitors can do this. The challenge is to produce loyal customers.

The need for customer retention

Unfortunately, most marketing theory and practice center on the art of attracting new customers rather than on retaining existing ones. The emphasis traditionally has been on making sales rather than building relationships; on preselling and selling rather than caring for the customer afterward. Some companies, however, have always cared passionately about customer loyalty and retention. The key to customer retention is customer satisfaction. A highly satisfied customer:

- Stays loyal longer
- Buys more as the company introduces new products and upgrades existing products
- Talks favorably about the company and its products
- Pays less attention to competing brands and advertising and is less sensitive to price
- Offers product or service ideas to the company
- Costs less to serve than new customers because transactions are routinized

Thus a company would be wise to measure customer satisfaction regularly. The company could phone recent buyers and inquire how many are very satisfied, indifferent, dissatisfied, and very dissatisfied. It might lose as much as 80 percent of the very dissatisfied customers, maybe about 40 percent of the dissatisfied customers, about 20 percent of the indifferent customers, and maybe 10 percent of the satisfied customers. But it may lose only 1 or 2 percent of its very satisfied customers. The moral: Try to exceed customer expectations, not merely meet them.

Some companies think they are getting a sense of customer satisfaction by tallying customer complaints. But, 95 percent of dissatisfied customers don't complain; many just stop buying. The best thing a company can do is to make it easy for the customer to complain. Suggestion forms and company toll-free numbers and e-mail addresses serve this purpose. The 3M company hopes that customers will call with suggestions, inquiries, and complaints. 3M claims that over two thirds of its product-improvement ideas come from listening to customer complaints. Listening is not enough, however. The company must respond quickly and constructively to the complaints.

Of the customers who register a complaint, between 54% and 70% will do business again with the organization if their complaint is resolved. The figure goes up to a staggering 95% to 96% if the customer feels that the complaint was resolved quickly. Customers who have complained to an organization and had their complaints satisfactorily resolved tell an average of five people about the good treatment they received. Because loyal customers account for a substantial amount of company profits, a company should not risk losing a customer by ignoring a grievance or quarreling over a small amount. IBM requires every salesperson to write a full report on each lost customer and all the steps taken to restore satisfaction. Winning back lost customers is an important marketing activity, and often costs less than attracting first-time customers.

Today, more and more companies are recognizing the importance of satisfying and retaining current customers. Here are some interesting facts bearing on customer retention.

- Acquiring new customers can cost five times more than the costs involved in satisfying and retaining current customers. It requires a great deal of effort to induce satisfied customers to switch away from their current suppliers.
- The average company loses 10 percent of its customers each year.
- A 5 percent reduction in the customer defection rate can increase profits by 25 percent to 85 percent, depending on the industry.
- The customer profit rate tends to increase over the life of the retained customer.

There are two ways to strengthen customer retention. One is to erect high switching barriers. Customers are less inclined to switch to another supplier when this would involve high capital costs, high search costs, or the loss of loyal-customer discounts. The better approach is to deliver high customer satisfaction. This makes it harder for competitors to overcome switching barriers by simply offering lower prices or switching inducements. The task of creating strong customer loyalty is called relationship marketing. Relationship marketing embraces all those steps that companies undertake to know and serve their valued customers better.

Task One Choose the best answer to fill in the blank.

1. _____ is a marketing term used, often in Internet Marketing, to describe the generation of consumer interest or inquiry into products or services of a business.
   A．Lead qualification   B．Lead elaboration
   C．Lead generation   D．Account conversion

2. _____ is the process of qualifying which of the suspects are really good prospects, and this is done by interviewing them, checking on their financial standing, and so on.
   A．Lead qualification   B．Lead elaboration
   C．Lead generation   D．Account conversion

3. The prospects may be graded as hot, warm, and cool. The sales-people first contact the hot prospects and work on _____ , which involves making presentations, answering objections, and negotiating final terms.
   A．lead qualification   B．lead elaboration
   C．lead generation   D．account conversion

4. His _____ as a film director has risen in recent years.
   A．living   B．role   C．standing   D．situation

5. The figures mentioned in the report _____ to every detail.
   A．conform   B．account   C．consist   D．tally

6. How do you _____ the company's alarmingly high staff turnover?
   A．account to   B．account with C．account about   D．account for

7. The company needs to improve its training and _____ of staff.

A．retain   B．retaining   C．retention   D．retainment

8. They offer every _____ to foreign businesses to invest in their country.

   A．inducement   B．bonus   C．perks   D．reward

Task Two　Decide whether the following statements are true or false according to the text.

1. （　　）Lead generation, lead qualification, and account conversion are the first three steps to attract new customers.

2. （　　）Today, the company did not worry about satisfying its customers, for customers may not have had many alternative sources of supply, or suppliers were equally deficient in service.

3. （　　）The challenge, according to Jeffrey Gitomer, is not to produce loyal customers; the challenge is to produce satisfied customers.

4. （　　）By tallying customer complaints is one of the most effective ways for some companies to get a sense of customer satisfaction.

5. （　　）Winning back lost customers is an important marketing activity, and often costs less than attracting first-time customers.

Task Three　Translate the following sentences from the text into Chinese.

1. Customer acquisition requires substantial skills in lead generation, lead qualification, and account conversion.

_____

_____

2. Today's customers are harder to please. They are smarter, more price conscious, more demanding, less forgiving, and approached by more competitors with equal or better offers.

_____

_____

3. Customers who have complained to an organization and had their complaints satisfactorily

resolved tell an average of five people about the good treatment they received.

_____

_____

4. Acquiring new customers can cost five times more than the costs involved in satisfying and retaining current customers.

_____

_____

5. Customers are less inclined to switch to another supplier when this would involve high capital costs, high search costs, or the loss of loyal-customer discounts.

_____

_____

Part C   Communication Values

Pre-reading Questions

➢ *What are the challenges presented by the nonverbal communication?*

➢ *List the major difficulties compromising an organization's attempt to communicate with customers in any location.*

Although English continues to grow in importance as the language of international travel and business, understanding and speaking the language of a country is an invaluable asset in understanding the country's culture. There is an often repeated maxim: You can buy in your home-country language, but you need to learn your customers' language to sell. The ability to communicate in our own language is, as most of us have learned, not an easy task. Whenever languages and culture change, additional communication challenges will present themselves. For example, "yes" and "no" are used in an entirely different way in Japanese than in Western languages. This has caused much confusion and misunderstanding. In English, the answer "yes" or "no" to a question is based on whether the answer is affirmative or negative. In Japanese, this is not so. The answer "yes" or "no" may indicate whether or not the answer affirms or negates the question. For example, in Japanese the question, "Don't you like meat?" would be answered "yes" if the answer is negative, as in, "Yes, I don't like meat." The word wakarimashita means both "I understand" and "I agree". To avoid misunderstandings, Westerners must learn to distinguish which interpretation is correct in terms of the entire context of the conversation. The box "A Matter of Culture: Getting Lost in Translation" shows other ways the verbal component of cross-cultural communication can get "lost in translation".

The challenges presented by nonverbal communication are perhaps even more formidable. For example, Westerners doing business in the Middle East must be careful not to reveal the soles of their shoes to hosts or pass documents with the left hand. In Japan, bowing is an important form of nonverbal communication that has many nuances. People who grow up in the West tend to be verbal, whereas those from the East are more nonverbal. Not surprisingly, there is a greater expectation in the East that people will pick up nonverbal cues and understand intuitively without being told. Westerners must pay close attention not only to what they hear but also to what they see, when conducting business in such cultures.

Communication experts generally agree that the overall requirements of effective communication and persuasion are fixed and do not vary from country to country. The same thing is true of the components of the communication process: The marketer's or sender's message must be encoded, conveyed via the appropriate channel(s), and decoded by the customer or receiver. Communication takes place only when meaning is transferred. Four major difficulties can compromise an organization's attempt to communicate with customers in any location:

- The message may not get through to the intended recipient. This problem may be the result of an advertiser's lack of knowledge about appropriate media for reaching certain types of audiences. For example, the effectiveness of television as a medium for reaching mass audience will vary proportionately with the extent to which television viewing occurs within a country.

- The message may reach the target audience but may not be understood or may even be misunderstood. This can be the result of an inadequate understanding of the target audience's level of sophistication or improper encoding.

- The message may reach the target audience and may be understood but still may not induce the recipient to take the action desired by the sender. This could result from a lack of cultural knowledge about a target audience.

- The effectiveness of the message can be impaired by noise. Noise in this case is an external influence such as competitive advertising, other sales personnel, and confusion at the receiving end, which can detract from the ultimate effectiveness of the communication.

The key question for global marketers is whether the specific advertising message and media strategy must be changed from region to region or country to country because of environmental requirements. Proponents of the "one world, one voice" approach to global advertising believe that the era of the global village is fast approaching and that tastes and preferences are converging worldwide. According to the standardization argument, because people everywhere want the same products for the same reasons, companies can achieve great economies of scale by unifying advertising around the globe. Advertisers who follow the localized approach are skeptical of the global village argument. Even Coca-Cola, the most global brand in the world, records radio spots in 40 languages with 140 different music backgrounds. Four Coca-Cola asserts that consumers still differ from country to country and must be reached by advertising tailored to the respective countries. Proponents of localization point out that most blunders occur because advertisers have failed to understand and adapt to foreign cultures. Nick Brien, managing director of Leo Burnett, explains the situation this way.

As the potency of traditional media declines on a daily basis, brand building locally becomes more costly and international brand building becomes more cost effective. The challenge for advertisers and agencies is finding ads which work in different countries and cultures. At the same time as this global tendency, there is a growing local tendency. It's becoming increasingly important to understand the requirements of both.

Task One Fill in the blanks with the expressions given below. Change the form when necessary.

. . . .

> encode; sophistication; maxim; impair; formidable; decode; converge; blunder; tailor to; potency

1. Several general strategies have been suggested for products; they are Quality Maxim, Quantity

Maxim, Relevance _____ , and Manner Maxim.

2. They are too evenly matched, and their natural differences are too _____ .

3. Currently, the homepage of Yahoo uses 33 kinds of different _____ cardinal number to generate.

4. He was frowning and wishing he could _____ the notations on the slips.

5. He combined curious qualities of naivete with incisive wit and worldly _____ .

6. All models do not own above functions, but the manufacturer can custom-_____ requirements.

7. Why Airbus and Boeing are more likely to _____ than to diverge?

8. His _____ would certainly queer his chances of promotion.

9. Plant sweet protein is a kind of high-_____ , low-caloric natural sweeteners.

10. The author's half drunken state did not in the least _____ his eminence in my eyes.

Task Two Choose the best answer according to the text.

· ·

1. The text mainly tells us that _____ .

   A. language plays an important role in business communication

   B. communication skills differ from country to country

   C. non-verbal communications present a formidable challenge in business

   D. the ability to communicate in our own language is not an easy task

2. The question "Don't you like meat?" in Japanese tries to tell us _____ .

   A. in English, the answer "yes" or "no" to a question is based on whether the answer is affirmative or negative

   B. in Japanese, the answer "yes" or "no" may indicate whether or not the answer affirms or negates the question

   C. to avoid misunderstandings, Westerners must learn to distinguish which interpretation is correct in terms of the entire context of the conversation

   D. "yes" and "no" are used in an entirely different way in Japanese than in Western languages

3. Which of the following is NOT one of the major difficulties an organization might confront when communicating with customers?

   A. The message may not get through to the intended recipient.

   B. The effectiveness of the message won't be influenced by external influence.

C. The message may reach the target audience but may not be understood or may even be misunderstood.

D. The message may reach the target audience and may be understood but still may not induce the recipient to take the action desired by the sender.

4. What does the Coca-cola case try to convey?

A. "One world, one voice" approach works.

B. The global tastes and preferences are converging.

C. Unifying advertising around the globe is workable.

D. As consumers differ from region to region, advertising must be tailored to countries.

5. A challenge for advertisers and agencies is _____ .

A. global tendency

B. a growing local tendency

C. traditional media

D. ways of communication effective in different cultural background

Task Three Sum up the main idea of the text in 100 words.

_____

_____

_____

_____

Part D Reading Strategy

Understanding Supporting Details

Supporting details give more information about the topic. They are not as general as the main idea. Instead, they help the reader understand more about the main idea. Different types of details are used to support different kinds of topics. For example, reasons and quotations are used to persuade, facts and statistics to explain, examples and steps to illustrate and anecdotes to emphasize or illustrate whatever point the author wishes to make.

Questions about supporting details are often checked in the following ways.

➢ According to the passage...

➢ The author states that...

➢ All of the following are mentioned in the passage/paragraph...EXCEPT...

➢ What does the passage say about?

➢ The author quotes to show...

Main types of supporting details

Type of Supporting Details	Example
Reasons （理由）	One obvious reward is the economy... The second benefit is... Last of all...
Facts or Statistics （事实或数据）	Indeed, the U. S. Bureau of Labor Statistics predicted in 1985 that jobs in the leisure and recreation services field would expand by 1.5 million over the next 10 years, a 27 percent increase.
Examples （实例）	A case in point is Paul, who was an excellent tennis player during his college years and won many medals and trophies.
Anecdotes （轶事）	When I was in short pants, I loved to color pictures in jumbo-sized coloring books. I even collected Crayola crayons and was eager to try out their new colors, such as the hot "Macaroni and Cheese".
Quotations （引文）	The old saying "All work and no play makes Jack a dull boy" seems to have merit.
Steps or Procedures （步骤）	To begin with, set aside a regular time for exercise... Next... Finally...

Fol l ow-up Work Read the article below quickly and choose the correct answer to each question.

∙ ∙

The decline in moral standards – which has long concerned social analysis – has at last captured the attention of average Americans. And Jean Bethke Elshtain, for one, is glad.

The fact that ordinary citizens are now starting to think seriously about the nation's moral climate, says this ethics professor at the University of Chicago, is reason to hope that new ideas will come forward to improve it.

But the challenge is not to be underestimated. Materialism and individualism in American society are the biggest obstacles. "The thought that 'I'm in it for me' has become deeply rooted in the national consciousness," Ms. Elshtain says.

Some of this can be attributed to the disintegration of traditional communities, in which neighbors looked out for one another, she says. With today's greater mobility and with so many couples working, those bonds have been weakened, replaced by a greater emphasis on self.

In a 1996 poll of Americans, loss of morality topped the list of the biggest problems facing the U.S. and Elshtain says the public is correct to sense that: Data show that Americans are struggling with problems unheard of in the 1950s, such as classroom violence and a high rate of births to unmarried mothers.

The desire for a higher moral standard is not a lament for some nonexistent "golden age," Elslhtain says, nor is it a wishful longing for a time that denied opportunities to women and minorities. Most people, in fact, favor the lessening of prejudice.

"Moral decline will not be reversed until people find ways to counter the materialism in society," she says. "Slowly, you recognize that the things that matter are those that can't be bought."

1. Professor Elshtain is pleased to see that Americans _____ .

   A．have adapted to a new set of moral standards

   B．are longing for the return of the good old days

   C．have realized the importance of material things

   D．are awakening to the lowering of their moral standard

2. Which of the following characterizes the traditional communities?

    A. Great mobility.   B. Concern for one's neighbors.

    C. Emphasis on individual effort.   D. Ever-weakening social bonds.

3. In the 1950s, classroom violence _____ .

    A. was something unheard of   B. was by no means a rare occurrence

    C. attracted a lot of public attention   D. began to appear in analysts' data

Part E Banked Cloze

Direction: *In the following text, there are ten blanks. Read the text and then fill in each blank with a word from the word bank. Each choice in the bank is identified by a letter. Do not use any of the words more than twice.*

Each time you try for a more responsible position, the selection process gets (1) _____ . Your abilities, personality traits, your lifestyle, values and aspirations will all be vigorously (2) _____ by your prospective colleagues and also your bosses. Do you know how to (3) _____ yourself when you are under the microscope? If you are to (4) _____ your ambitions, now is the time to learn how to do (5) _____ to yourself and prepare for formal selection processes. Learn about the various methods you can employ to find your way into a different institution, gain a more sophisticated (6) _____ of how headhunters work and learn to position yourself so that you can be found easily. Taking (7) _____ of any situation to maximize your visibility is very useful. Even when you are not offered a particular job for which you have been considered, do leave an impression which will remain in the mind of the headhunter should other possibilities (8) _____ . You (9) _____ it to yourself to do the best you can. Make sure you perform in such a way that you can be satisfied that the decision about you has been made with the (10) _____ amount of up-to-date and accurate information about your capabilities. Do you know what they are and do you have some stories prepared which will illustrate them well?

A) greatest B) arise C) understanding D) handle E) tougher F) justice G) owe
H) scrutinized I) realize J) advantage

Unit 11

Business Management

Part A Brainstorming

Directions: *Read the following short story and then discuss the following questions.*

➢ *How did the fox know that the sick lion ate all the disappeared beasts?*

➢ *What can you learn from the story in the perspective of business management?*

The Sick Lion

A Lion, unable from old age and infirmities to provide himself with food by force, resolved to do so by artifice. He returned to his den, and lying down there, pretended to be sick, taking care that his sickness should be publicly known. The beasts expressed their sorrow, and came one by one to his den, where the Lion devoured them.

After many of the beasts had thus disappeared, the Fox discovered the trick and presenting himself to the Lion, stood on the outside of the cave, at a respectful distance, and asked him how he was. "I am very middling," replied the Lion, "but why do you stand without Pray? Enter within to talk with me." "No, thank you," said the Fox. "I notice that there are many prints of feet entering your cave, but I see no trace of any returning."

What can you learn from the story?

A. He is wise who is warned by the misfortunes of others.

B. Nature exceeds nurture.

C. Birds of a feather flock together. .

D. United we stand, divided we fall.

Part B Corporate Planning

Pre-reading Questions

➢ *What does corporate planning mean?*

➢ *Define the major competitive scopes within which the company will operate.*

Defining the corporate planning

An organization exists to accomplish something: to make cars, lend money, provide a night's lodging, and so on. Its specific planning or purpose is usually clear when the business starts. Over time the planning may lose its relevance because of changed market conditions or may become unclear as the corporation adds new products and markets to its portfolio.

When management senses that the organization is drifting from its planning, it must renew its search for purpose. According to Peter Drucker, it is time to ask some fundamental questions. What is our business? Who is the customer? What is of value to the customer? What will our business be? What should our business be? These simple-sounding questions are among the most difficult the company will ever have to answer. Successful companies continuously raise these questions and answer them thoughtfully and thoroughly.

Organizations develop planning statements to share with managers, employees, and (in many cases) customers. A well-worked-out planning statement provides employees with a shared sense of purpose, direction, and opportunity. The statement guides geographically dispersed employees to work independently and yet collectively toward realizing the organization's goals. Planning statements are at their best when they are guided by a vision, an almost "impossible dream" that provides a direction for the company for the next 10 to 20 years. Sony's former president, Akio Morita, wanted everyone to have access to "personal portable sound", so his company created the Walkman and portable CD player. Fred Smith wanted to deliver mail anywhere in the United States before 10:30 a. m. the next day, so he created Federal Express.

Here are two examples of planning statements:

Rubbermaid Commercial Products Inc.: Our Vision is to be the Global Market Share Leader in each of the markets we serve. We will earn this leadership position by providing to our distributor and end-user customers innovative, high-quality, cost-effective and environmentally responsible products. We will add value to these products by providing legendary customer service through our Uncompromising Commitment to Customer Satisfaction.

Motorola: The purpose of Motorola is to honorably serve the needs of the community by providing products and services of superior quality at a fair price to our customers; to do this so as to earn an adequate profit which is required for the total enterprise to grow; and by so doing provide the opportunity for our employees and shareholders to achieve their reasonable personal objectives.

Good planning statements have three major characteristics. First, they focus on a limited number of goals. The statement "We want to produce the highest-quality products, offer the most service, achieve the widest distribution, and sell at the lowest prices" claims too much. Second, planning statements stress the major policies and values that the company wants to honor. Policies define how the company will deal with stakeholders, employees, customers, suppliers, distributors, and other important groups. Policies narrow the range of individual discretion so that employees act consistently on important issues. Third, they define the major competitive scopes within which the company will operate:

Industry scope: The range of industries in which a company will operate. Some companies will operate in only one industry; some only in a set of related industries; some only in industrial goods, consumer goods, or services; and some in any industry. For example, DuPont prefers to operate in the industrial market, whereas Dow is willing to operate in the industrial and consumer markets. 3M will get into almost any industry where it can make money.

Products and applications scope: The range of products and applications that a company will supply. St. Jude Medical aims to "serve physicians worldwide with high-quality products for cardiovascular care".

Competence scope: The range of technological and other core competences that a company will master and leverage. Japan's NEC has built its core competences in computing, communications, and components. These competences support its production of laptop computers, television receivers, and handheld telephones.

Market-segment scope: The type of market or customers a company will serve. Some companies will serve only the upscale market. For example, Porsche makes only expensive cars and licenses its name for high-quality sunglasses and other accessories. Gerber serves primarily the baby market.

Vertical scope: The number of channel levels from raw material to final product and distribution in which a company will participate. At one extreme are companies with a large vertical scope; at one time Ford owned its own rubber plantations, sheep farms, glass manufacturing plants, and steel foundries. At the other extreme are corporations with low or no vertical integration. These "hollow corporations" or "pure marketing companies" consist of a person with a phone, fax, computer, and desk who contracts out for every service including design, manufacture, marketing, and physical distribution.

Geographical scope: The range of regions' countries, or country groups in which any will operate. At one extreme are companies that operate in a specific or state. At the other extreme are multinationals such as Unilever and Caterpillar, which operate in almost every one of the world's countries.

Planning statements should not be revised every few years in response to every new turn in the economy. However, a company must redefine its planning if that planning has lost credibility or no longer defines an optimal course for the company. Kodak has redefined itself from a film company to an image company so that it could add digital imaging. IBM has redefined itself from a hardware and software manufacturer to a "builder of networks." Sara Lee is redefining itself by outsourcing manufacturing and becoming a marketer of brands.

Task One Choose the best answer to fill in the blank.

1. He claims that the laws are antiquated and have no contemporary _____.

    A. relation   B. connection   C. relevance   D. reference

2. We will actively manage your _____ to maximize the return on your investment.

    A. combination   B. portfolio   C. investment   D. management

3. As rural factories shed labor, people _____ towards the cities.

A．wander B．roam C．float D．drift

4. When the boss falls from power，his lackeys _____．

A．disperse B．spread C．scatter D．distribute

5. _____ to the documents remains restricted to civil servants.

A．Way B．Entry C．Approach D．Access

6. _____ in speech is more than eloquence.

A．Valor B．Caution C．Discretion D．Bravery

7. The big six record companies are multinational，and thus can _____ the world market into national ones.

A．segment B．portion C．division D．section

8. What is the _____ mix of private and public property rights in natural resources?

A．optimum B．optimal C．glory D．glorious

Task Two Decide whether the following statements are true or false according to the text.

1. (　　) The planning may lose its relevance due to changed market conditions or the addition of new products and markets to its portfolio.

2. (　　) Good planning statements have three major characteristics.

3. (　　) Policies widen the range of individual differences so that employees act consistently on important issues.

4. (　　) Planning statements should be revised every few years to accommodate to every new turn in the economy.

5. (　　) A company must redefine its planning if that planning has lost credibility or no longer defines an optimal course for the company.

Task Three Translate the following sentences from the text into Chinese.

1. Over time the planning may lose its relevance because of changed market conditions or may become unclear as the corporation adds new products and markets to its portfolio.

2. When management senses that the organization is drifting from its planning, it must renew its search for purpose.

_____

_____

3. The statement guides geographically dispersed employees to work independently and yet collectively toward realizing the organization's goals.

_____

_____

4. We will earn this leadership position by providing to our distributor and end-user customers innovative, high-quality, cost-effective and environmentally responsible products.

_____

_____

5. A company must redefine its planning if that planning has lost credibility or no longer defines an optimal course for the company.

_____

_____

Part C Globalization

Pre-reading Questions

➢ *Why did markets and marketing win out in the competition with communism?*
➢ *Is the trade cycle relevant to companies today? Why? Why not?*

The rise of global markets

The trend that will change the future of global marketing is the rise of global market segments. Today, more than ever before, there are global segment opportunities. In category after category, global efforts succeed. For example, the soft-drink industry was first successful in reaching a global cola segment and has now moved to address the fast-growing fruit-and-flavor segment.

There are global segments for luxury cars, wine and spirits, every type of medical and industrial product, teenagers, senior citizens, and enthusiasts of every stripe and type, from scuba divers to snowboarders.

The rapidly growing diffusion of Internet access combined with the rapidly expanding bandwidth and capacity of the global Internet itself will play a major role in supporting the growth of global markets and global marketing. Amazon. com can reach customers in Taiwan and Tokyo just as easily as it can reach customers in Boston. Customers anywhere in the world are only a click away from the book of their choice. With express mail service, customers are only two days away from delivery wherever they live, and with credit cards they can pay for goods and services in any currency.

These are the new economic realities. The rich are getting richer, the poor in many countries are getting richer faster, and the world economy is becoming more and more integrated. This means new opportunities and new challenges for companies and countries.

What is the future for the average consumer? The possibilities are unlimited. How about high-tech "pets" to care for the elderly? Matsushita Electric has developed "pets," which record the number of times their owners talk to them or hold them. This information is transmitted to an agency that monitors these elderly. The pet "can respond to a greeting, engage in simple conversation and even express remorse when scolded." In every field, from medicine and health care to transportation to information technology to entertainment to retailing, there will continue to be revolutionary changes.

The rise of Internet and information technology

Perhaps the most significant of all of the changes impacting global marketing is the rise of the Internet and information technology (IT). Marketing, for the first time in history, can address the individual customer. Before the Internet, the smallest marketing segment was a group or cluster of customers with similar needs. Today, marketing has the tools to address the segment of one, the individual customer and his or her needs.

This capability is available to address markets from local to global. In addition, companies can for the first time really focus on the customer. Today, small companies can act like large companies, and large, giant companies can act like small companies. This is energizing every sector of the global economy, especially in the high-income countries that have the resources to invest in IT. In addition to e-commerce, the Internet revolution is creating a new medium for information, entertainment, communication, advertising and a new e-commerce retail segment.

Summary

The future of global marketing will reflect five major changes in world growth but with some major new directions. The growth of Southeast Asia has been interrupted. That region now offers exceptional risk and reward equations for global marketers who are willing to make a bet on the long-term potential of the region. The cost of market entry has dropped as dramatically as the decline in values of national currencies. For companies with a stomach for risk, there is an opportunity to invest, building market positions in countries that most experts believe will soon return to long-term growth. In the mean time, other world regions will continue to grow, and world wealth will become more evenly distributed.

The trade cycle has not eliminated manufacturing as a source of employment and income in the high-income countries. By investing in capital equipment and by designing products for manufacturability, rich countries have proven that they continue to successfully compete as manufacturing locations.

Global markets will continue to grow in importance as global marketers continue their quest to identify and serve global segments. This growth will enhance and expand the value of global experience for managers and executives worldwide.

Finally, marketing is at the threshold of a new and exciting era: E-business, E-commerce, and E-marketing. For the first time in history, marketers have the tools to address the needs of the individual customer.

Task One Fill in the blanks with the expressions given below. Change the form when necessary.

. . . .

> *address*；*category*；*cluster*；*diffusion*；*energize*；*eliminate*；*equation*；*segment*；*threshold*；
> *executive*

1. Designer wedding dresses make wedding fashion a separate _____ from mainstream fashion.

2. Throughout the book we have _____ ourselves to the problem of ethics.

3. The big six record companies are multinational，and thus can _____ world market into national ones.

4. Acupuncture has a harmonizing and _____ effect on mind and body.

5. The invention of printing helped the _____ of learning.

6. There's no town here，just a _____ of shops，cabins and motels at the side of the highway.

7. The availability of public transport is also part of the _____.

8. The sound was so loud it was on the _____ of pain.

9. CEO stands for chief _____ officer.

10. Liu Xiang is _____ from the London Olympics in the first round.

Task Two Choose the best answer according to the text.

. . . .

1. What does the text mainly talk about?

   A . The rise of the global market segments will be a trend in the future.

   B . There're great demands for products on global level.

   C . Global markets will continue to grow in importance.

   D . The most significant of all of the changes impacting global marketing is the rise of the Internet and information technology.

2. "Amazon. com can reach customers in Taiwan and Tokyo just as easily as it can reach customers in Boston." indicates _____.

   A . the trend that will change the future of global marketing is the rise of global market segments

   B . there are global segments for many kinds of products

   C . the rapidly growing diffusion of Internet access plays a major role in supporting the growth of global markets

   D . the growth of market worldwide will enhance and expand the value of global experience for businessmen

3. Which of the following is NOT one of the features of "pets"?

   A . Pets refer to those gadgets which record the number of times their owners talk to them or hold them.

   B . Pets are exclusively designed for the trendsetters.

   C . It would transmit some information to an agency that monitors these elderly.

D. Pets can respond to a greeting, engage in simple conversation and even express remorse.

4. "Finally, marketing is at the threshold of a new and exciting era." What does "the threshold" mean?

A. The smallest detectable sensation.

B. A region marking a boundary.

C. The sill of a door; a horizontal piece of wood or stone.

D. The starting point for a new state or experience.

5. Why does the author say "Marketing, for the first time in history, can address the individual customer."?

A. This capability is available to address markets from local to global.

B. Companies can for the first time really focus on the customer.

C. The most significant of all of the changes impacting global marketing is the rise of the Internet and information technology.

D. Small companies can act like large companies, and large, giant companies can act like small companies.

Task Three Sum up the main idea of the text in 100 words.

· ·

_____

_____

_____

_____

· ·

Part D Reading Strategy

Identifying the Author's Purpose

When an author writes, he always has a purpose in mind. Identifying the author's purpose helps readers to understand the ideas presented in the text better. In order to tell whether an author is writing to persuade, inform, or entertain, readers should first learn about two types of writing:

Non-fiction: Non-fiction is about real facts or events rather than imagined things. Texts may be persuasive, informative, descriptive or instructive. Through this type of writing, the author may inform, give directions, illustrate, or present information.

Fiction: Fiction is about imaginary people or events such as short stories or novels. This type of writing is usually written to entertain, to express one's feeling and emotions, or to meet the reader's aesthetic needs.

How can one identify the author's purpose in a non-fiction text? Non-fiction texts usually include histories, biographies, newspaper and magazine articles, as well as how-to manuals. When reading texts, one should ask himself the following questions to help identify the author's purpose.

➤ Is the author trying to inform the reader about something?

➤ Is the author trying to explain something?

➤ Is the author trying to persuade the reader?

➤ Dose the author have a hidden agenda?

Ultimately, these questions will help determine the purpose of a specific text.

Fol I ow-up Work   Read the short paragraphs carefully and identify the author's purpose.

· ·

Paragraph 1

But is it legal? Are you risking criminal charge or a civil lawsuit by taping your sitter? The answer is yes to the first question; your nanny cam, in most instances, is perfectly legal. However, there are still a few details which should be brought to your attention and discussed with an attorney licensed in your state if you have additional questions.

The author's purpose is _____

_____

Paragraph 2

Animal cloning is the process by which an entire organism is reproduced from a single cell taken from the parent organism and in a genetically identical manner. This means the cloned animal is an exact duplicate in every way of its parent; it has the exact same DNA. Cloning happens quite frequently in nature. A sexual reproduction in certain organisms and the development of twins from a single fertilized egg are both instances of cloning. With the advancement of biological technology, it is now possible to recreate the process of animal cloning artificially.

The author's purpose is _____

_____

Paragraph 3

Have you seen *Jurassic Park*? In this feature film, scientists use DNA preserved for tens of millions of years to clone dinosaurs. They find trouble, however, when they realize that the cloned creatures are smarter and fiercer than expected. Could we really clone dinosaurs? In theory, yes. What would you need to do this?

➢ A well-preserved source of DNA from the extinct dinosaur?

➢ A closely related specious, currently living, that could serve as a surrogate mother.

In reality, probably not. It's not likely that dinosaur DNA cloud survive undamaged for such a long time. However, scientists have tried to clone species that became extinct more recently, using DNA from well-preserved tissue samples.

The author's purpose is _____

_____

Part E Banked Cloze

Directions: *In the following text, there are ten blanks. Read the text and then fill in each blank with a word from the word bank. Each choice in the bank is identified by a letter. Do not use any of the words more than twice.*

Corporate planning may be described as the careful and systematic taking of strategic decisions. In contrast to a short-term plan like a budget, a corporate plan is concerned with taking a long-term (1)_____ of future developments and with designing a strategy so that the organization can achieve its chosen objectives. Many large companies now recognize the importance of (2)_____ a formal approach to developing a corporate plan. They prepare 'scenarios' or forecasts of future developments in the (3)_____ in which they wish to operate, in order to examine whether decisions taken in the present will result in success in the future. In recent years, companies have been developing more sophisticated (4)_____ with which to analyze the risks involved in such decisions.

(5) _____ , for example, an oil company deciding if it should invest in a new refinery. Faced with this decision, involving the (6)_____ of millions of pounds on something which might have a life of 15 years or more, the company must have a sound basis for its decision. In this case, it needs to know whether it can be (7)_____ of a market for the extra volume of its refined products, and it needs to know whether they can be produced profitably. In addition, it is necessary to study the (8) _____ of crude oil and other supplies needed in the process.

Corporate planning, therefore, involves three main areas: (9)_____ the long-term objectives of an organization, deciding what market (10) _____ there may be and formulating a product policy to satisfy them.

A) consider   B) environment   C) determining   D) assured   E) view   F) techniques
G) availability   H) potential   I) investment   J) outlay

Unit 12

Management Innovation

Matrix

- Entrepreneurship
- Managing research and development project

Part A   Brainstorming

Directions: *Read the following short story and fill in the blank. And then discuss the following questions.*

....

➢ *Is the student clever or innovative?*

➢ *Do you stand with the student?*

A college student was in a philosophy class, where a class discussion about whether or not God exists was in progress.

The professor had the following logic: "Has anyone in this class heard God?"

Nobody spoke.

"Has anyone in this class touched God?"

Nobody spoke.

"Has anyone in this class seen God?"

When nobody spoke for the third time, he simply stated, "Then there is no GOD."

A student did not like the sound of this at all, and asked for permission to speak. The professor granted it, and the student stood up and asked his classmates the following questions:

"Has anyone in this class heard our professor's brain?"

Silence.

"Has anyone in this class touched our professor's brain?"

Absolute silence.

"Has anyone in this class seen our professor's brain?"

When nobody in the class dared to speak, the student concluded, "Then, according to our professor's logic, _____ "

The following information may do help to expand your thinking perspective:

1. Is the professor's logic right?

2. What does the student want to prove?

Part B　Entrepreneurship

Pre-reading Questions

➢ *How to distinguish between invention and innovation?*

➢ *What is the role entrepreneurship plays in a company?*

Innovation and Entrepreneurship

A global study by the Boston consulting group in 2005 showed that large global companies worldwide want to increase their spending on innovation. These executives concurred, to a large degree, that generating growth through innovation is essential for success in their respective industries. Furthermore, these executives indicated they were not satisfied with their return on investment to date for innovation. Some of their concerns with innovation are in the area of how to move quickly from idea generation to commercialization and initial sales, how to leverage suppliers for new ideas, and how to properly balanced risk, time frames, and returns.

It is important to distinguish between invention and innovation. Invention is the creation of new products or processes through new knowledge or the integration of existing knowledge in new ways. Innovation is the initial commercialization or dissemination by other means of invention, by producing and selling a new product, service or process. Innovation requires controls and discipline to bring these novel inventions to practical use for customers.

Innovation is a powerful concept that is seen by many as the future of business, a sort of holy grail, silver bullet or panacea, especially in a knowledge-based economy. We can define entrepreneurship as the undertaking of a venture, seizing of opportunities to generate a valuable product or service and bring its completion. Furthermore, entrepreneurship can be seen particularly as the creation of something new that changes or transmutes values, opening a new space for human action or interaction.

We can characterize entrepreneurial endeavors as being those activities which involve the entrepreneurial characteristics of vision, ownership and passion. So the question is how can these entrepreneurial activities and mindsets be introduced to, and be allowed to play themselves out, within the context of a corporate culture. There are many aspects of corporate culture which actually work against the successful implementation of entrepreneurial visions.

So an innovative product or service is devised to satisfy the needs of target customers who can be considered stakeholders. From an industry standpoint, we can talk about products, services, technologies, processes, expertise, strategies and other innovative opportunities. We can also apply this industry model and apply it to the government, education, military and the arts. These new ways of organizing flow from matching innovation and entrepreneurship. They can be very powerful means to deliver solutions that can improve many aspects of our lives.

In fact, some argue that there is no business without entrepreneurship; that the actual act of organizing a business or producing a product or launching a new corporate strategy is in fact an entrepreneurial undertaking. Usually we reserve the term entrepreneurship to refer strictly to the creation of new ventures. However the strategy guru Gary Hamel defines strategy as revolution. He argues that you're not doing strategy if you're not breaking the rules or inventing new rules: in other words, engaging in an essentially entrepreneurial venture.

This offers a new-era definition of strategy, one that inextricably links strategy with innovation and entrepreneurship. Think of Apple Computer's iPad as a strategy revolution: a business model innovation that integrated the converging industries of recorded music, computers, and consumer-electronics into a portable music device. It took the entrepreneurial innovation of arguably the master technology strategist of the 20th century, Steve Jobs, to invent a business model that integrated these diverse industries and solved a perplexing industry problem. Previous to that, the best thinking of the top management of the music industry was to sue 12-year-olds for digital music file sharing- hardly an inspiring example of entrepreneurial innovation at the corporate level.

So, we can think of entrepreneurs bringing about innovation of new business undertakings within an existing organization, whether that organization operates in government, industry, education, military, arts or even religion. This is usually referred to as intra-preneurship. The term intra-preneur is used less frequently now because we have recast our notion of what it means to be any employee of a company. Due to downsizing, reengineering, outsourcing, and a corporate strategy often designed around using consultants rather than employees, now, in the 21st century, most employees appropriately think of themselves as "hiring out their services to a given firm for a given period of time". They see themselves essentially a self-employed, similar to an entrepreneur who runs an owner-managed business. So the term intra-preneurship has fallen away to some extent, while the notion that we are all entrepreneurs on some level, has gained greater currency.

Task One   Choose the best answer to fill in the blank.

1. He might feel that _____ the company at a time when he sees tremendous growth opportunities would be a mistake.

   A. helping   B. financing   C. leveraging   D. providing

2. Western aid may help but will not be a _____.

   A. medicine   B. drug   C. cure   D. panacea

3. Medieval alchemists attempted to _____ base metals into gold.

   A. change   B. transmute   C. turn   D. morph

4. As a disciple, one must regard one's _____ as an enlightened being.

   A. teacher   B. instructor   C. guru   D. president

5. The solid, ordinary candidate responds as 'a passionate customer champion and _____'.

   A. employee   B. worker   C. innovator   D. intrapreneur

6. Free-market reforms have moved governments everywhere to _____, deregulate, and privatize.

   A. downsize   B. upsize   C. diminish   D. minimize

7. Do what you do best (your core competency) and _____ the rest!

   A. delegate   B. outsource   C. automate   D. package

8. The idea has acquired a proverbial _____.

   A. currency   B. belief   C. saying   D. proverb

Task Two Decide whether the following statements are true or false according to the text.

. . . .

1. (   ) Invention is the initial commercialization (or dissemination by other means) of invention.
2. (   ) Controls and discipline are required to bring inventions to practical use.
3. (   ) Entrepreneurship can be referred to those activities involving vision, ownership and passion.
4. (   ) The needs from stakeholders determine the functions of innovative product or service.
5. (   ) The term entrepreneurship refers strictly to the creation of new ventures.

Task Three Translate the following sentences from the text into Chinese.

. . . .

1. These executives concurred, to a large degree, that generating growth through innovation is essential for success in their respective industries.

_____

_____

2. Invention is the creation of new products or processes through new knowledge or the integration of existing knowledge in new ways.

_____

_____

3. Innovation is the initial commercialization (or dissemination by other means) of invention, by producing and selling a new product, service or process.

_____

_____

4. We can characterize entrepreneurial endeavors as being those activities which involve the entrepreneurial characteristics of vision, ownership and passion.

_____

_____

5. Due to downsizing, reengineering, outsourcing, and a corporate strategy often designed around using consultants rather than employees, now, in the 21st century, most employees appropriately

think of themselves as "hiring out their services to a given firm for a given period of time."

_____

_____

Part C   Managing Research and Development Project

Pre-reading Questions

➢ *What are the roles R&D plays in the strategy making of a company*?

➢ *What are the three types of organizational approaches*?

R&D organizations are structured in different ways. Through the time companies have either centralized or decentralized them. Today we see a combination of both worlds existing. Central R&D labs generally look two to three product generations ahead. That is about 5 to 10 years. Decentralized labs are closer to the business units and they tend to focus on 2 – 5 year or 1 product generation ahead.

Companies have realized that there is a need for both types of R&D units. Intel Corporation, for example, is organized that way. There is a central R&D organization called "Corporate Technology Group". Its focus is 5 – 10 years from today and they explore several ideas that may turn into profitable products. On the other hand, R&D units within business units are focused on the next generation product line. The same structure exists in other organizations such as Samsung and IBM.

In addition to the internal organization, linkages with the external world are very critical in managing an R&D organization. One of the major roles of the R&D organizations is to provide technology intelligence. So it is required for these organizations to establish external networks. Companies such as Samsung, IBM and Intel have established such networks to funnel in technology intelligence. In the case of Intel, there are four major mechanisms.

- The first one is university grants. Intel and other companies are using university grants to be able to have access to university research and to monitor developments. These grants are generally three years long and usually support the cost of a PhD student.

- The second major mechanism is university labs. These represent higher cost and require physical space reserved in the campus under the name Intel Labs. There are six of them around the world.

- The third mechanism consists of internal strategic projects that can be proposed by Intel employees.

- The final mechanism is called Intel Capital. It involves buying stakes in companies owning technologies that have the potential to impact Intel's business (in either direction).

Through these four mechanisms, Intel establishes a very wide network of technology intelligence, then making up for the disadvantage of being a large corporation with a risk of missing the early indicators of emerging disruptive technologies.

In the last decade corporate R&D has seen a drastic change. Both internal and external organization structures are required for effective R&D management. Another factor that is critical is the rigidity of these organizations. One thing that is certain in managing R&D is nothing is certain-that is uncertainty is the major attribute of R&D. Therefore organizations and managers need to be able to deal with ambiguity in managing the R&D programs.

Generally there are three types of organizational approaches: functional, project and matrix.

- Functional organizations are concentrated single functional groups managed by functional managers reporting to a senior manager.

- On the other hand, project organizations are multifunctional groups tasked with a project reporting to a project manager.

- Matrix organizations are a hybrid of both functional and project forms, in which projects matrix across the functional groups. Members from functional organizations are assigned to projects temporarily and go to other projects when their assignment is over. Members of the projects in this case report both to their functional manager and the project manager.

The degree of uncertainty should play into the selection of the approach. For example, a program that is similar to one that was undertaken recently would be handled through a matrix organization, whereas a program involving a new manufacturing process would probably be more successful if a project organization is used. On the other hand, for sustaining operations such as taking care of product issues after the launch of the product (for example), functional organization would be the best.

Moving, merging and spinning organizations may be required at the end of an R&D project. If a project team is working on a brand new technology which the company had ever dealt with in the past, it would have a hard time to find a team that could productize it within the company. There would be a need for company-wide training, and this would take long time. In these cases companies may choose to take the whole team and make them responsible for product development as well. They can be either a stand-alone team or merged into an existing product development team. Merger would be useful as the team coming from the technology world would be familiar with the product constraints as well as the product team is. Another option would be to spin out a company if the technology is considered radically different, or even to form alliances with other companies to productize it.

Task One Fill in the blanks with the expressions given below. Change the form when necessary.

· ·

---

constraint; merge; alliance; initiative; compatible; aggregate; grant; funnel; matrix; initiative; spin out

---

1. Its Global Program on AIDS _____ money from donors to governments.
2. France has agreed to _____ him political asylum.
3. What is needed, as one executive described it, is a " _____ of mutually supportive goals".
4. Please _____ all these items together under the item of " incidental expenses ".
5. We felt a little _____ with the new boss for the first day or so.
6. The two parties entered into a defensive _____ with each other to win the election.
7. Foreign bankers and economists cautiously welcomed the minister's _____ .
8. Their objectives were _____ with the interests of North American investors.
9. The tax increases will, in the _____ , cause much hardship.
10. I'll try to _____ my money in order to make both ends meet at the end of every month.

Task Two Choose the best answer according to the text.

. . . .

1. What is the subject of the passage?

   A. R&D organizations are structured in different ways.

   B. There is a great need for both centralized and decentralized labs.

   C. How to manage R&D programs through collaboratively different organizations.

   D. Moving, merging and spinning organizations are required in an R&D project.

2. Linkages with the external world are very critical in _____.

   A. establishing networks to funnel in technology

   B. turning ideas into profitable products

   C. providing technology intelligence

   D. focusing on the next generation product line

3. Which of the following is NOT of organizational approaches?

   A. Functional organizations.   B. Project organizations.

   C. Matrix organizations.   D. Research organizations.

4. Which of the following is NOT for the improvement of technology intelligence?

   A. Offering grants for the excellent university students.

   B. Setting up labs in famous universities around the world.

   C. Buying the advanced technologies from other companies or countries.

   D. Providing enough capital needed.

5. What should NOT a project team do if it is working on a brand-new technology?

   A. Company-wide training.

   B. The responsibility for product development from the whole team.

   C. Merger.

   D. Isolation from other companies.

Task Three Sum up the main idea of the text in 100 words.

. . . .

_____

_____

Part D Reading Strategy

Summarizing

Summarizing is a short statement that contains your own interpretation of what you have read. It usually includes the main idea and the major details. A good summary should reflect briefly and accurately what the author has said. To achieve that purpose, you must decide what the author's intention is and recollect only essential information. Be cautious not to distort the main idea or omit any significant point.

Here are some of the main steps in making a summary:

➢ Be familiar with the material that you are reading. Consider the main idea and the organizational pattern of the whole passage.

➢ Write out the main idea in complete sentences.

➢ Find important information that supports your statement.

➢ Be brief. Get rid of extra words in your summary to emphasize the essential information.

➢ Read the whole summary to make sure it flows smoothly and includes all important points.

Fol l ow-up Wor k **Read the following passage and write a summary of it.**

There are roughly three New Yorkers. There is, first, the New York of the man or woman who was born here, who takes the city for granted and accepts its size and its turbulence as natural and inevitable. Second, there is the New York of the commuter – the city that is devoured by locusts each day and spat out each night. Third, there is the New York of the person who was born somewhere else and came to New York in quest of something. Of these three trembling cities the greatest is the last – the city of final destination, its poetical deportment, its dedication to the arts, and its incomparable achievements. Commuters give the city its tidal restlessness, natives give it solidity and continuity, but the settlers give it passion. And whether it is a farmer arriving from Italy to set up a small grocery store in a slum, or a young girl arriving from a small town in Mississippi to escape the indignity of being observed by her neighbors, or a boy arriving from the Corn Belt with a manuscript in his suitcase and a pain in his heart, it makes no difference: each embraces New York with the fresh eyes of an adventurer, each generates heat and light to dwarf the Consolidated Edison Company.

Summary of the passage.

_____

_____

_____

Part E Banked Cloze

Directions: *In the following text, there are ten blanks. Read the text and then fill in each blank with a word from the word bank. Each choice in the bank is identified by a letter. Do not use any of the words more than twice.*

Stressful working conditions lead to a breakdown in group co-operation which can damage effectiveness and productivity, a study has found. Psychologists have discovered that when employees work in crisis (1)_____, they are less willing to work together. The study showed that when workers are under stress, they have a strong (2)_____ to concentrate on their own personal (3)_____ to the detriment of their colleagues. In the study, 100 naval personnel worked in groups of three, and each group was given a computer (4)_____ of a naval decision-making task. Under a high (5)_____ of stress, they had to monitor a radar screen with their own ship at the centre and numerous unidentified contacts around the ship. As (6)_____, participants operating in this highly stressful situation performed worse than those operating under normal circumstances. But the results also showed that under stress, the workers' (7)_____ of attention shifted from group involvement to a more narrow individual perspective, which led to a severe breakdown in team performance.

The author of the study concludes that it is possible that, for many team tasks, the importance of teamwork behavior such as co-ordination and communication may be (8) _____ as secondary to basic individual demands. In his opinion, the (9) _____ to achieve efficiency under stress is by delegation. Simplifying tasks by delegating parts of them, making them less demanding, is one of the best ways of (10) _____ the effectiveness of the group.

A) expected　B) tendency　C) way　D) goals　E) conditions　F) degree　G) maintaining
H) focus　I) simulation　J) perceived

Appendix

1. Reference

［1］ 孔蕴华、吴立高.国际财务金融英语教程(教师用书.下册)［M］.北京:经济科学出版社,2010

［2］ 孔蕴华、吴立高.国际财务金融英语教程(学生用书.下册)［M］.北京:经济科学出版社,2010

［3］ 格林.剑桥商务英语考试(BEC)历年真题解析及模拟试题(中级)［M］.北京:中国石化出版社,2011

［4］ 肖云南.商务英语选读——泛读［M］.北京:清华大学出版社;北京交通大学出版社,2010

［5］ 王晓光.大学商务英语阅读［M］.上海:华东理工大学出版社,2008

［6］ 王茹、胡燕.秘书英语［M］.北京:中国人民大学出版社,2011

［7］ 张立玉.实用商务涉外礼仪［M］.北京:北京理工大学出版社,2009

［8］ http://www.ehow.com/how_5134819_arrange-travel.html

［9］ http://www.northeastern.edu/adminm/hrm/ep/resignation.htm

［10］ http://www.citeman.com/12974-internal-mobility-and-transfer.html

［11］ http://www.investopedia.com/articles/01/110701.asp♯axzz28DqMAdr1

［12］ http://www.investopedia.com/articles/03/060403.asp♯axzz28DqMAdr1

［13］ http://dict.cn/

［14］ http://www.iciba.com/

2. Keys for reference

Unit 1

Part A

Prepare three envelopes!

Part B

Task One 1-8 CBAD BCBA

Task Two 1-5 FFTTT

Task Three

1. 然而,还是有很多文件需要印出来,以纸质形式传达,特别是需要签字的文件。

2. 除非是要该收件人处理某事,否则不需要将之放在收件人一栏中(接受邮件)。

3. 作为传抄中的收件人,发件人并不希望你就信件中涉及的主题发表看法,只是礼节性地告知你而已。

4. 这就是说你想要某人知晓邮件的信息,但你又不希望别的收件人知晓某人也收到了该邮件。

5. 如果你是唯一的收件人,那你收到该邮件后,就应该及时处理该邮件。

Part C

Task One

1. engage in

2. executive/administrative

3. liaise with

4. administrative

5. assertive

6. competency

7. payroll

8. clerical

9. integrity

10. coordinator

Task Two 1-5 BDCCB

Part D　Reading Strategy

The answer depends on individual prediction.

Part E

1 – 10　BEDFA　HJGCI

Unit 2

Part A

anyone who is working

Part B

Task One　1 – 8　BDCB　ACBB

Task Two　1 – 5　FTFTT

Task Three

1. 办公室管理可以确保办公室工作标准,维护工作程序,及时纠正偏差。

2. 员工如欲请假,需填写员工请假单,并附上请假的详细理由。

3. 办公室工作人员有义务为自己和他人的健康着想。

4. 办公室压力通常包括三类:工作压力,心理压力和技术压力。

5. 技术压力包括:培训不足;工具设备老化或保养不善;工作量过大;缺乏良好的工具设备;工具设备设计不佳,缺乏安全性。

Part C

Task One

1. acknowledge

2. isolation

3. confidential

4. mutual

5. contribution

6. disapprove of

7. executive

8. Nevertheless

9. take advantage of

10. efficiency

Task Two　1 – 5　CBDAB

Part D   Reading Strategy

Task One

1. Scientific research is like an exploration or a voyage of discovery. You are continually trying out new things that have not been done before.

2. One of the best things about scientific research is that you are always doing something different and it is never boring.

Part E

1 – 10   HCAIG   JBFDE

Unit 3

Part A

（Dearest Wife：

Just got checked in. Everything prepared for your arrival tomorrow.）

Part B

Task One   1 – 8   CDCB   ADCA

Task Two   1 – 5   FFTFT

Task Three

1. 只有当文件管理系统高效的时候办公室工作才能运转正常。

2. 相关记录不论是以原始的纸张形式还是经过处理的电子稿形式,都应该正确存放以便能及时获取。

3. 可以节省因在大量文件和纸张中寻找信息而浪费掉的时间。

4. 在电脑化的文件管理系统中,可以使用不同类型的软件来储存信息,如数据库和空白表格程序。

5. 当断电或系统崩溃时将无法获取信息。

Part C

Task One

1. suspicious

2. switch off

3. shredder

4. breach

5. regularly

6. duplicate

7. leaked

8. warning off

9. lest

10. potential

Task Two 1 – 5 BCDBA

Part D Reading Strategy

1. She carried out her studies of college students by comparing their college entrance exam scores with grade point averages.

2. Students with the cheerleading parents showed less anxiety about challenges; lower anxiety was linked to more self-confidence, which predicated better grades.

   Having supportive friends or romantic partners didn't affect grade point average.

3. College students whose parents always assured them they were able scholars earn higher grades than classmates with the same academic ability but less supportive parents.

Part E

1 – 10 FAIDB JCHEG

Unit 4

Part A

A

Part B

Task One 1 – 8 BADB BDAC

Task Two 1 – 5 TFTTT

Task Three

1. 最关键的议题是如何让普通员工关心公司所说的话。

2. 员工需要在三个层面接受信息,即:语境层面,战略层面和个人层面。

3. 为什么众多的高层管理人员对内部交流投入时间和财力会感到困难重重呢?

4. 这项研究发现,从统计数字上看,员工积极的情绪和公司五年股东的红利之间有重要的联系。

5. 公司在这一点上普遍犯的错误是使用一刀切的方法。

Part C

Task One

1. portrays

2. primary

3. incentive

4. self-esteem

5. motivate

6. retaliatory

7. merit

8. challenges

9. induce

10. tension

Task Two 1 – 5 CDABB

Part D   Reading Strategy

Passage 1

1 – 8 ABAC BCAA

Passage 2

1 – 8 AABB BACA

Part E

1 – 10 CJGAB IEHFD

Unit 5

Part A

make two copies

Part B

Task One 1 – 8 ABCB BCBB

Task Two 1 – 5 FTTTT

Task Three

1. 你可能见过或亲身经历过这种讨价还价，但坦白地说，除了这种半威胁半恳求的拉锯战也没有什么好办法了。

2. 但是还有另外一种处理方式，可以较快地达成结果并减少摩擦，即基于需求的谈判。

3. 大多数精明的商人不会告诉你他们买你商品愿意出的最高价格，除非他们不打算跟你做这笔生意了。

4. 这次交易最重要的不是卖给你这个商品，而是在今后一年中一系列的后续交易。

5. 毕竟，告诉你他的需求确实能让你尽快地作出一个符合他需求的报价，而不用拐弯抹角。

Part C

Task One

1. agenda

2. Refreshments

3. duplicates

4. advisable

5. defined

6. circulated

7. destructive

8. distributes

9. press

10. capacity

Task Two 1－5 DCDCB

Part D Reading Strategy

1. skilled；logical relationship/antonym

2. disagree；antonym

3. magazine；example

4. insult；synonym

5. a difficult situation；restatement

6. independence；common sense

7. tired；cause and effect

8. a person who own and run their own small businesses；definition

9. disturbed；restatement

10. unhelpful；antonym

Part E

1－10 JBFDG CAHIE

Unit 6

Part A

with my luggage in the trunk

Part B

Task One 1－8 BBDA CADB

Task Two 1－5 TTFFF

Task Three

1. 当你计划一次商务旅行时,你可以搜寻最好的航线,使旅行安排既便宜又舒适。

2. 把你的联运交通安排在飞机降落后几个小时,能使你避免带着行李来一次穿越机场的五英里慢跑。

3. 如果你是一名飞行常客,选择一家航线覆盖你大部分常规目的地的航空公司,并且加入其飞行常客计划。

4. 如果你是短途旅行,轻装简行,带上笔记本电脑和随身携带的行李箱就够了。

5. 这会精简你的旅行安排,减轻你商务旅行途中更多的压力。

Part C

Task One

1. countless

2. converse

3. daunting

4. assessing

5. thrilled

6. cancellations

7. amusement

8. budget

9. historical

10. refundable

Task Two   1 – 5   DACCD

Part D   Reading Strategy

Topic of passage:Improving your English

Topics of the paragraphs:

1. using methods to improve English

2. improving vocabulary by using a dictionary

3. looking up new words in a dictionary

4. reading poetry aloud

5. keeping a journal or blog

6. long-term benefits of improving English

Part E

1 – 10   EDAJC   BFHGI

Unit 7

Part A

A

Part B

Task One   1 – 8   ACBC   DBAD

Task Two 1-5 FFFFT

Task Three

1. 打算自愿辞职的员工应该向他们的主管或部门领导递交辞呈,详细说明辞职的原因和工作的最后一天。

2. 主管也应该为员工提供一份离职信息,由于员工即将离开公司,这份离职信息对他们而言包含着重要的信息。

3. 由于裁员而收到停职通知的员工要去人力资源管理部门寻求帮助,寻找他可能胜任的其他合适公司空岗。

4. 如果员工的工作表现继续处在标准水平之下,那么,主管应该进一步找他谈话,给予警告和咨询,并且该部门应该咨询人力资源管理部门。

5. 在这样的情况下,部门领导必须咨询相关的副总裁和人力资源管理部门,以便概括出明确的行动方案。

Part C

Task One

1. effectiveness

2. assignment(s)

3. fluctuate

4. promotion

5. utilize

6. mobility

7. transfer

8. relief

9. versatile

10. ensure

Task Two 1-5 DBDAC

Part D Reading Strategy

passage 1 B

passage 2 B D

Part E

1-6 GABFEC

Unit 8

Part A

B

Part B

Task One 1 - 8　BCCC　BDDC

Task Two 1 - 5　FFTTT

Task Three

1. 根据被服务人数划分每个项目的真正成本,由此,你也能够分析出每个服务单位的成本。

2. 尽管无法预测的事件可能会影响到费用和贡献,你仍然可以根据过去的经验相对准确地估算出收益。

3. 为更为保守或乐观的收益规划制定应急预算也很可以解燃眉之急。

4. 当然,巨额财政赤字会导致破产,而且大量过剩意味着该组织没有把足够的收益投入到服务公众利益上。

5. 如果初步预算已准备妥当,而收益与开销的关系不理想,那么,计划和管理行为就必须重新评估并做出调整。

Part C

Task One

1. exceed

2. accrue

3. financial

4. accounting

5. assets

6. lubricant

7. shed light on

8. in the long run

9. compress

10. equivalents

Task Two 1 - 5　BDCCC

Part D　Reading Strategy

Passage 1

1. When　2. However　3. First　4. Second　5. because

Passage 2

1. Firstly　2. Secondly　3. like　4. Thirdly　5. Therefore

Part E

1 - 6　FCIHDG

Unit 9

Part A

is your first worry

Part B

Task One　1－8　BCCC　BDDC

Task Two　1－5　FFTTT

Task Three

1. 直接成本将包括以下费用：篮子、篮中物品、篮子包装和将篮子组合在一起的劳动。

2. 一旦你知道所卖的每件产品或每次服务的卖价和直接成本，你就能以美元算出每件物品的贡献毛利。

3. 你要知道经营你的公司要花费多少钱，因为在盈利前，你除了支付直接成本，还要支付这些开销。

4. 提高定价和尽力削减成本可能只是提高让你继续经营的贡献毛利和盈利。

5. 你需要将算出的盈亏平衡点融入到定价政策中，以确保你卖的每件产品都盈利，并且你能根据成本和卖价获得利润。

Part C

Task One

1. discrepancies

2. transaction

3. disposal

4. debit

5. current

6. remittance

7. exchange

8. capital

9. inheritance

10. extraction

Task Two　1－5　BDCCC

Part D　Reading Strategy

1. C　2. D

Part E

1－6　AFDEBG

Unit 10

Part A

Yes，I'd be an office boy at Microsoft!

Part B

Task One 1-8 CADC DDCA

Task Two 1-5 TFFFT

Task Three

1. 获得客户需要根本技能,包括发现潜在客户,甄别潜在客户以及转化潜在客户。

2. 今天的客户更难以满足。他们更精明,对价格更计较,要求更高,更不宽容。他们周围有着来自更多竞争厂商所提供的等同或更好质量的产品。

3. 那些向厂商抱怨,并且得到满意回复的顾客们平均下来会告诉他们的五个伙伴他们得到了多好的待遇。

4. 开发新客户的成本是满足并留住现有客户成本的五倍之高。

5. 当涉及到高资金成本、高开发成本,或是原有忠实客户折扣的失去,客户们不太愿意转而购买另一个供货商的产品。

Part C

Task One

1. Maxim

2. formidable

3. encode

4. decode

5. sophistication

6. tailor to

7. converge

8. blunder

9. potency

10. impair

Task Two 1-5 BCBDD

Part D Reading Strategy

1. D   2. B   3. A

1. D   问题为细节记忆题。   2. B   问题为细节判断题。   3. A   问题为细节辨认题。

1－10　EHDIF　CJBGA

Unit 11

Part A

A

He is wise who is warned by the misfortunes of others.（聪明人懂得以他人的不幸为鉴）

Nature exceeds nurture.（本性难移）

Birds of a feather flock together.（物以类聚，人以群分）

United we stand，divided we fall.（团结就是胜利，分裂必然失败）

Part B

Task One　1－8　CBDA　DCAB

Task Two　1－5　TTFFT

Task Three

1. 由于市场多变，计划可能失去相关性；或者因公司推出新产品，挖掘新市场，原有计划变得模糊。

2. 当管理层意识到结构正在偏离计划时，它必须有目的地更新其研究。

3. 此申明指导不同地区员工既独立又协力地实现公司共同目标。

4. 我们将通过提供给分销商以及最终用户以创新、高品质、划算的环保产品来确保领先地位。

5. 如果原有计划失去可信度，或不能为公司提供最优途径，公司必须重新定义其计划。

Part C

Task One

1. category

2. addressed

3. segment

4. energizing

5. diffusion

6. cluster

7. equation

8. threshold

9. executive

10. eliminated

Task Two　1－5　ACBDB

Part D   Reading Strategy

Paragraph 1

The author's purpose is to advise those who are concerned about legal issues to consult a lawyer before using a nanny cam.

Paragraph 2

The author's purpose is to give the readers a brief introduction to the way animal cloning is done.

Paragraph 3

The author's purpose is to discuss the possibility of cloning extinct species such as dinosaurs.

Part E

1 - 10   EJBFA   IDGCH

Unit 12

Part A

it must be true that our professor has no brain!

Part B

Task One   1 - 8   CDBC   DABA

Task Two   1 - 5   FTTTF

Task Three

1. 这些行政官员一致同意在很大程度上，通过创新来增长对其各自产业有着很重要的作用。

2. 发明是指通过新知识或者使用新方法对已有知识的整合，从而创造出新产品或者新方法。

3. 创新是发明的初步商业化(或者说传播)，它生产和销售新产品，新服务和新的加工方法。

4. 我们用企业家特有的眼界、所有权和热情所创造的活动来描绘企业家精神。

5. 由于缩小规模，重新改造，外包服务，外加顾问型而非雇员型的公司战略，21 世纪大部分雇员能正确地意识到自己只是在某个特定时期受雇于某个特定的企业。

Part C

Task One

1. funnelled

2. grant

3. matrix

4. merge

5. constraint

6. alliance

7. initiative

8. compatible

9. aggregate

10. spin out

Task Two　1 ~ 5　CCDCD

Part D　Reading Strategy

Summary of the passage:

　　The above passage discusses three New Yorks: that of the native, the commuter, and the newcomer. The newcomers arrive in New York from different places and for different reasons and they contribute to the city's excitement, energy and achievements.

Part E

1 ~ 10　EBDIF　AHJCG

图书在版编目(CIP)数据

涉外秘书英语阅读/莫玉羚,周红宇主编.—上海:华东师范大学出版社,2013.3
高校涉外秘书专业系列教材
ISBN 978 - 7 - 5675 - 0458 - 5

Ⅰ.①涉⋯ Ⅱ.①莫⋯②周⋯ Ⅲ.①秘书-英语-阅读教学-高等学校-教材 Ⅳ.①H319.4

中国版本图书馆 CIP 数据核字(2013)第 053516 号

涉外秘书英语阅读

总 主 编	杨剑宇	
副总主编	冯修文	
主 编	莫玉羚 周红宇	
项目编辑	姚 望	
审读编辑	王 英	

出版发行　华东师范大学出版社
社　　址　上海市中山北路 3663 号　邮编 200062
网　　址　www.ecnupress.com.cn
电　　话　021 - 60821666　行政传真 021 - 62572105
客服电话　021 - 62865537　门市(邮购)电话 021 - 62869887
地　　址　上海市中山北路 3663 号华东师范大学校内先锋路口
网　　店　http://hdsdcbs.tmall.com

印 刷 者　苏州工业园区美柯乐制版印务有限公司
开　　本　787×1092　16 开
印　　张　11
字　　数　243 千字
版　　次　2013 年 8 月第一版
印　　次　2013 年 8 月第一次
书　　号　ISBN 978 - 7 - 5675 - 0458 - 5/H·620
定　　价　30.00 元

出 版 人　朱杰人